The Afro-Asian States
and Their Problems

**BY K. M. PANIKKAR**

*Asia and Western Dominance*
*In Two Chinas*
*The Founding of the Kashmir State*
*India and the Indian Ocean*

K. M. PANIKKAR

# The Afro-Asian States
## and
## their Problems

*Ruskin House*
GEORGE ALLEN & UNWIN LTD
MUSEUM STREET LONDON

*First published 1959*

*Second Impression 1959*

*This book is copyright under the Berne Convention. Apart from any fair dealing for the purpose of private study, research, criticism, or review, as permitted under the Copyright Act, 1956, no portion may be reproduced by any process without written permission. Enquiries should be addressed to the publisher.*

© *George Allen & Unwin Ltd. 1959*

*Printed in Great Britain
in 10pt. Pilgrim type
by
East Midland Printing Company Limited
Bury St. Edmunds, Peterborough, Kettering
and elsewhere*

## AUTHOR'S NOTE

The Institut d'Étude de Developpement Economique et Social, of the Sorbonne, invited me to deliver six lectures on the problems of the newly independent States of Asia and Africa. The present volume is a slightly summarised version of these lectures. I am grateful to the authorities of the University for the honour they conferred on me in inviting me to deliver these lectures.

# CONTENTS

| | | |
|---|---|---|
| INTRODUCTION | | page 11 |
| I | *Political Structure* | 15 |
| II | *The Problems of Administration* | 31 |
| III | *The Problems of Economic Life* | 44 |
| IV | *Education* | 57 |
| V | *Science in the New States* | 69 |
| VI | *The Social Problems of the New States* | 81 |
| | INDEX | 97 |

# INTRODUCTION

THE period between 1945 to 1957 witnessed the independence of many States in Asia and Africa. India, Pakistan, Burma, Indonesia, Ceylon, Vietnam, Cambodia and Laos in South and South-East Asia emerged from their colonial position and became sovereign States. In the Middle East Syria and Lebanon became members of the international community after the exclusion of French authority from the area. Egypt, though technically a sovereign state before, was able to liquidate the occupation finally only in 1953 with the withdrawal of the British forces from the Canal base. In 1955 the Sudan became independent, and in the year following the French withdrew from Tunisia and Morocco. In 1957 Ghana achieved the status of a Dominion in the Commonwealth. Thus from Indonesia to Morocco on the Atlantic coast a new community of Asian and African nations, who had been in the nineteenth and the first half of the twentieth century under the political authority of European nations had been liberated from their tutelage and became responsible for shaping their own destinies.

The problems that these countries face, on becoming independent, are in many ways similar. In area, population, structure of society, natural resources and industrial capacity they vary very greatly. India has a population of three hundred and eighty millions, while Lebanon and Jordan each claimed just over a million. Similar is the case in respect of natural resources. If the differences between these new States are in many ways striking there is also a great similarity in the problems that face them. They have had in every case to build up a political organisation. Their own traditional political structures had disappeared during the period of their subjection and new

## Afro-Asian States

institutions had, therefore, to be built up. The administrative services necessary for a modern government had also to be provided. Their economy, formerly adjusted to the policies of the metropolitan government, had to be reorganised. The social system, which had been in most cases outside the purview of the colonial government, had to be modernised. In fact the new States, on achieving their independence, realised for the first time the immense responsibilities which they had to face.

The period during which these States recovered their independence and emerged as members of the international community (1945-1957) was itself revolutionary in the widest sense and this fact shaped their structure and determined their problems. The bomb that fell at Hiroshima not only sounded the death knell of an age but proclaimed a new era in world history which had been shaping during the previous half century. The rapid and revolutionary changes in science inaugurated by Planck's discovery had begun to transform almost every aspect of human life. The isolation of countries broke down completely, with the conquest of air and the range and power of weapons. The world had become in effect a single entity. The nineteenth and the first quarter of the twentieth century had undoubtedly given the impression of a unity to the world but that unity had been based on the supremacy of European and Western nations over the rest of mankind. It was superficial and political. The emerging unity of the period following 1945 is different in character as the social and industrial structure of the world and the interdependence of people have become much more definite and are clearly in the process of an evolution, when the differences which were once considered fundamental are being gradually obliterated. Everywhere this process could be seen. Knowledge and science are universal in their character and, as never before, they have become the com-

## Introduction

mon heritage of mankind. Mass communication has enabled ideas to penetrate the most backward regions, and though their effects may vary according to the state of evolution in each community, there is no doubt that today no country can live on the ideas of the past.

There are three major aspects of this change which need to be emphasised. The first is the revolutionary change in the conception of the community constituting the state. In the nineteenth century, and indeed till quite late into the twentieth century, the community and the state were identified with classes which enjoyed political and economic power, generally based on land in most countries outside the great industrial nations of the West. Today the community has become coextensive with the totality of adult population including women. The organisation of state has, therefore, become fundamentally different from what it had been in the past. Secondly, the nature of industrial production has undergone changes which none could have foreseen half a century ago. The new industrial revolution which the world is witnessing is in many ways different in character from its forerunner in the eighteenth and nineteenth century, so far as its complexity, its dependence on continuous research, its requirements of human and financial potential and its effect on society are concerned. Not only has technology to be widespread but scientific knowledge has to be shared by an ever increasing percentage of population in order to enable the industrial revolution to move forward. Thirdly, the social changes which have taken place during this short period are such as to make the period before the second World War look like a forgotten *ancien régime*. In the new States of Asia this is very much more apparent. The Confucian family, the marriage system and the class relationships in China which had been considered the special characteristics of the social organisation of

## Afro-Asian States

that country have changed beyond recognition during the last ten years. In India the personal law of the Hindus under which 350 million people had lived for over 2,500 years has been changed. The abolition of the system of untouchability, the legalisation of marriages between castes, the breakdown of the joint family, these are changes brought about not only by the social urges of today but by the new attitude towards the State, community and economic production.

It is thus into a new world that these States of Asia and Africa were born. Their problems were determined for them. The fact that during the preparatory era of this great revolution these States were under the foreign control intensified the nature of the problem. By and large the effects of the first industrial revolution had passed over them without fundamentally altering the structure of their society. Broadly speaking, the industrial growth of the European nations had only helped to subordinate the economic life of the countries to the interests of the metropolis. Their political organisation was dominated by the countries which ruled over them. Their educational and scientific skills had only been inadequately developed. Their resources had not been organised to meet the changed conditions. The new States had thus to face the problems of a great revolutionary age into which they were thrust—problems of unexampled complexity—without an adequate political and administrative organisation, without essential skills and technical equipment, and also without a social preparation which could release the energies of the community to deal with the problem of transformation. What is attempted in the lectures that follow is to indicate some of the problems which the new States of Africa and Asia face in these revolutionary circumstances.

# Political Structure

FOLLOWING the acquisition of independence, every State in Asia and Africa (except Libya) became a republic and opted for democracy. Neither a republican form of government nor democratic institutions based on elected representation had a genuine local tradition in any of the countries where they were thus transplanted. It is true that in India at one time in the distant past there flourished many republics of considerable size and importance. Equally it is a historical fact that the principle of decision by majority was well established in the Buddhist *sangha* many centuries before Christ. But these traditions had disappeared long ago, and the dominant and almost exclusive tradition of political organisation everywhere in Asia and Africa was monarchical and non-democratic. Nor is there anything surprising in this. In Europe itself before the first Great War monarchy was the normal form of political structure. Everywhere in Europe except in France (and in Portugal) the monarchical form continued to be accepted as legitimate and normal. In Germany, Austria, Russia and Spain, ancient dynasties claimed to rule by divine right and were highly suspicious of democratic institutions. In England, Holland, Belgium and the Northern countries, no doubt a compromise had been worked out, but the forms continued to be monarchical. To such an extent was monarchy considered the normal form that so late as 1911, when it was decided to make Albania independent, the great powers undertook a search for a suitable candidate

## Afro-Asian States

for the 'mbretship' of that country. It is only after the first Great War, when the Romanoffs, Habsburgs and the Hohenzollerns ceased to rule, and the Ottomans were deposed, that the idea became prevalent that countries achieving independence in the old world need not be supplied with monarchs of suitable status.

Nor could it be claimed that even after the war democracy had gained universal acceptance even in Europe. In the inter-war period, the major countries of Europe outside England, Switzerland and France and the Northern States had all of them deliberately chosen an autocratic, totalitarian form of government. It was not merely that Hitler and Mussolini had denounced democracy as a degenerate form of government, but everywhere, Salazar in Portugal, Metaxas in Greece, Ataturk in Turkey, Dollfuss in Austria, Franco in Spain and Piloudski in Poland, with varying degrees of popular support, denied the basic conceptions of democracy and established forms of government which, if not in all cases Fascist, were authoritarian.

It is significant, therefore, that when the States of Asia and Africa achieved their independence they should have elected to become republics and provided themselves with constitutions which were at least democratic in form. To some extent this was due to the influence of the metropolitan countries, whose institutions naturally appeared to the subject countries as models to be followed. Thus the countries which formed part of the British Empire adopted mainly the forms of English parliamentary government, while in Indonesia the conditions of the Dutch system were reproduced. Also, there was undoubtedly the desire of the political leadership of these countries to be considered modern and progressive, and in view of the fact that democracy had regained its prestige as a result of the second World War, there was no immediate attempt either to set up new monarchies or to experiment

## Political Structure

with semi-Fascist regimes, as had been the case in the Asian countries during the period of Japanese sponsored independence.

The choice of a republican democratic form of government by the new States (other than protectorates like Cambodia, Laos, Morocco and Tunisia which recovered their authority) was a major decision of far-reaching consequence, involving many problems which require careful study. Though as a result of the fact that they were born into a revolutionary era, they have, as we have already noted, to face many problems of unusual complexity, the problems of democratic organisation stand on a different footing, as they affect all other aspects of their political life; their stability and efficiency and indeed their very existence.

Each one of these States during the last ten years has attempted to work a representative form of government with cabinets, parliaments and other paraphernalia of democracy. And yet it is clear that in most cases the full implications of this system of government have not been understood, not only by the people but by the leaders themselves. Their previous experience has not been generally related to democratic methods of government or administration. In most cases the psychological background necessary for a government by the people was also absent.

The basic problem in a democracy is what may be called the doctrine of obedience. So long as the political structure was monarchical the problem was simple. Everyone knew that the monarch had to be obeyed. He was hedged with 'majesty', power, dignity and all other symbols of authority, that to the people he was the embodiment of the State. His will was the law. His whims were commands. The orders of the Emperor of China ended with the formula 'tremble and obey' and the people did tremble and

*Afro-Asian States*

obey because monarchical authority was complete and covered every aspect of life. The sanctions available to the monarch were absolute.

By long tradition the monarch's right to exact obedience was accepted almost as axiomatic. There is a very interesting discussion in the great Hindu epic, the *Mahabharata*, about the duty of obedience to a king. The question was posed as to why the king should be obeyed when he had only two eyes, two arms, etc., like any other man. The answer is interesting. If there is no visible final authority in a State, man will fall back to a state of anarchy which is picturesquely described as the *Matsyanyaya* or the law of the fish, that of the big fish eating the smaller ones. An ultimate authority to which obedience is due is clearly necessary if any kind of social organisation is to function. Its most easily understood form was that of a wise and powerful individual, chief or king, who was endowed both with a mystique of power and glory, and with the necessary sanctions. He became, in due course, Augustus, Son of Heaven, Tsar, the All Highest, invested not only with the totality of power but with almost superhuman majesty. To disobey him was the greatest offence. This was a principle which was easy to understand. But none of the countries which became newly free after 1945 (except Libya) opted for a monarchical form of government.

The problem of obedience was, in their case, formally determined by the practices and conventions existing in democratic States. In a democracy the final authority is, in theory, vested in the will of the people; in practice it is vested in the decision of the majority in parliament. A decision taken by the majority is held to be like the decision of a sovereign ruler, though, in federal constitutions, its legality could be questioned in a court of law. It is not open to be challenged by any other authority, or by

## Political Structure

any individual. But the finality of such decisions is not quite such an easy principle for everyone to understand. It is today one of the assumptions of democratic government that majority decisions should be accepted and obeyed. But it has not always been so. The librum veto in Poland was, perhaps, an unusual procedure. But even today in the Security Council it is the rule of the unanimity of the great powers that prevails and this would appear to be a clear violation of the alleged sanctity of majority decision. Even in democratic parliamentary systems, a special majority is sometimes provided in respect of specified matters: for example, for constitutional amendment a majority of two-thirds is generally provided or even a reference to the sovereign will of the people by a referendum. It is obvious from these examples that there is nothing axiomatic about the idea that a majority decision should always be accepted.

Also, even in the most advanced democratic countries there are institutions meant to limit the power of transient majorities to take important decisions. Most countries enjoying parliamentary government have a Senate, a House of Lords or some other kind of a second chamber, the object of which is to limit the power of a majority to impose its decisions in haste, even when such chambers have no overriding powers.

When the problem is so complicated even in well established democracies, it needs no argument to prove that in the new States the right of a majority to exact obedience meets with unexpected difficulties. The recent rebellion in Indonesia, the chronic disobedience of organised groups in Burma and the recent changes of regime by extra parliamentary methods in Syria provide the best examples. What emerges from these facts is that except in India, Ceylon and Pakistan, the decisions of parliaments have been defied by groups, based either on military power or

## Afro-Asian States

a claim to local independence. Nowhere outside the three countries, India, Pakistan and Ceylon[1], could it be said that the problem of obedience in a democratic system has found a solution.

The successful working of parliamentary democracy is dependent on a number of 'conventions' or generally accepted codes of political conduct, the free functioning of organisations which are opposed to the policies of Government, an independent Press, and an acceptance of the rule of law. Of these undoubtedly the most important, which has made the rule of majority the norm of parliamentary life, is the recognition that an independent opposition is as much a part of the democratic form of government as majority rule. In a democratic country it is not only that the opposition is tolerated but is to be considered a necessary part of the democratic machinery, entitled by every legitimate means to secure the confidence of the electors and become transformed into government. In fact what differentiates a democracy from other systems of government is the existence of an opposition. It is only where the opposition to the government in power has defined rights and duties, enjoys prestige and has complete freedom that 'a majority rule' can claim obedience.

Neither an absolute monarchy nor a totalitarian government can afford to recognise an 'official' opposition. Under a truly monarchical government opposition to the will of the monarch is sedition and may easily become treason. There is a well authenticated story of an autocratic potentate visiting the House of Commons and exclaiming, when he found that the orator whose speech was being applauded was the Leader of the Opposition, that in his

---

[1] Since these lectures were delivered, democracy has been replaced by military dictatorship in Pakistan also.

The defiance of parliamentary decisions by the Federal Party in Ceylon would seem to indicate that there also the question is to a large extent unsolved.

## Political Structure

country the man would have been executed. In totalitarian countries, also, no public opposition to the régime was ever permitted. When dictators experimented with opposition the fate of Adnam Bey provided a grim warning.

A second feature of democracy—indeed its essential characteristic—is the association of the people with the government at all levels. A democratic government does not come into existence merely because there is an elected central parliament and even a cabinet responsible to it. It is a question of the democratic process functioning at all levels, in the districts, in municipalities and in all other institutions concerned with the government of the people. One of the major difficulties which the newly independent States had to face was that in many of them these popular institutions did not exist at the lower levels. This is one of the chief differences between the States of Europe and the newly independent States of Asia and Africa. Among the many new States of Asia only in the old Indian Empire was there a considerable tradition of democratic local self government. As early as 1883 Lord Ripon established in India a system of local and municipal administration which provided the country with a democratic basis for its future development. Long before the Central Legislature became a democratic parliament the municipal and district authorities had worked the democratic system and familiarised the country with its assumptions. But such an experience was lacking in Indonesia and the Arab countries freed from the Ottoman rule.

A third factor which affects the functioning of democracy in the new States is the lack of independent thinking connected with political problems. Democratic institutions provide only a machinery of political action; its leadership has of necessity to be concerned with the day to day problems of administration and with the for-

*Afro-Asian States*

mulation of general policies. But it does not generate ideas. Even in the most advanced democratic countries, like England, France and the USA, the ideas which shape policies are not generated in Parliament. When such ideas have gained certain popularity and strength in the country they are *reflected* in Parliament, and finally come to be adopted as official policies. Prof. A. V. Dicey, in his well known work entitled *Legislation & Public Opinion in England in the 19th Century*, demonstrated that every single piece of major legislation passed in England during that important period had been fought out in the country before it came up for legislation in Parliament. Democracy, in fact, has to be provided with ideas. In every democratic country there is a process of co-operative thinking which is continuously going on, being debated, argued about and studied in detail. Institutions like the Fabian Society, through many years, brought to public issues a body of trained thought. Today the leading political parties maintain their own institutions of research. But more important than such professional researchers are groups with special interests studying national problems, discussing them and providing public men with ideas concerning every aspect of national life.

The role of Universities and higher educational institutions in providing the ideas and doctrines of democratic policies needs also to be emphasised. Though in the nineteenth century the great democratic reforms were the outcome of public agitations, the arsenal of ideas was provided by the intellectuals of an earlier age. In pre-revolutionary Europe the Universities had fallen from their high estate and the leadership of thought had passed to independent groups like the Encyclopaedists in the eighteenth century, and to men like Humboldt, Stein and others in Germany and to the utilitarians in England in the early nineteenth century. One of the remarkable features of the

## Political Structure

growth of democracy in England, France and America has been the re-emergence of Universities as vital centres of political thought. Their influence has radiated not only from specialised institutions like the London School of Economics and the Ecole des Sciences Politiques, but also from discussion groups and clubs formed around leading academic personalities. In recent years this has been a notable feature of University activities in England, France and the USA, where, apart from active encouragement of discussions and seminars on questions of public importance, many foundations for regular research into such problems have come into existence.

Unfortunately most of the new countries are ill equipped for such intellectual work in the political sphere. In most of these countries outside India and Pakistan, Universities and higher educational institutions are only now beginning to be established. In Ceylon, Burma, Malaya, Indonesia, Iraq, Syria, etc., the Universities are only a few years old and have not yet established a tradition of independent work. In India, where the tradition of modern Universities is now a hundred years old, there has been some notable activity in this field and institutions like the Delhi School of Economics, the Gokhale School of Politics (Poona), Institute of Public Administration and the research courses connected with the Calcutta, Bombay and Madras Universities have been engaged in some work of this nature. *Ex hypothesi* in the period of colonial authority such work could not have been undertaken, as independent political thinking was the last thing which colonial authorities could afford to encourage.

The importance of independent political thinking in democratic government cannot be over-emphasised. Parliamentary democracy by its very nature is government by gentlemen amateurs. In this it differs from the monarchical system which, for example, during the Cameralist

## Afro-Asian States

régimes of the German monarchs of the eighteenth century could draw upon the talents of experts for the purposes of government. Also the doctrine of parliamentary democracy in the days of its development was one of *laissez faire*. It is only during the last fifty years that democracy discarded this tradition and began, under the pressure of Socialist thinking, to engage actively in programmes of political, economic and social well-being. The ideas for these vast programmes of national welfare and growth were provided at all times by the voluntary intellectual activity of dynamic groups.

This remains the basic problem of democracy in the new States. There is everywhere a paucity of personnel outside the government for important work of this kind. Governments themselves are expanding organisations. Their activities tend to extend in every direction. Such *elite* as the new States have is, in many cases, hardly sufficient to man the government itself. In many of these States, even for normal administration, governments have had to depend on outside assistance. Consequently, for the essential work of thinking out the problems which face the new States and for providing solutions for them in terms of local conditions, there is but little talent available. Therefore in most of these States democracy remains a borrowed ideology, whose implications are little understood and whose institutions have no special significance.

The significance of this point will be clear when it is realised that democratic processes and functions were developed in very special political backgrounds, with the result that the institutions through which people's sovereignty is realised differ from country to country. Democracy in France has many characteristics which are absent in the parliamentary government of England. The two party system, the powers of the Cabinet in deciding the business of Parliament, the rights and functions of the

## Political Structure

Opposition and many other features of the British system are foreign to the temper of France. Equally, the system of parliamentary permanent committees, cabinets based on agreement between groups, the practical independence of the conseil d'etat, and the wide powers of the Civil Service are features of the French system which seem strange from the English point of view. The Presidential system of America with the executive authority vested in a single person elected by the suffrage of the nation and with independent judicial and legislative authorities, differs from both the British and French systems and is equally democratic. There is clearly no uniformity in democratic systems and it is, therefore, necessary to understand what the essential factors are which constitute a democratic system. The new States have in the main copied their institutions from the metropolitan power which ruled them without making any effort to distinguish between what is essential and what is incidental. They have, in fact, become text book democracies, with but little relation, in most cases, to the social and economic conditions of the countries concerned. The consequence is that in many of them there is an air of unreality —an attitude of make-believe. In two of the leading States, Pakistan and Indonesia, the heads of States themselves have made public declarations about their lack of faith in democratic institutions. More than once President Mirza of Pakistan has declared himself in favour of a form of 'guided democracy', while President Sukarno of Indonesia has been experimenting with a system of 'controlled democracy'. In Pakistan, though up to the present (1958) no general election has been held, and a Constitution was promulgated only in 1956, no less than Seven Ministries had held office at the Centre, and it had been frankly recognised that the process by which Ministries had come into being or had fallen has seldom conformed to demo-

## Afro-Asian States

cratic practices. The case of Premier Nazim-ud-Din was particularly revealing. He was the head of a political party which at the time enjoyed the confidence of parliament. The budget which his government presented had been passed by parliament with a comfortable majority, and yet the Governor-General dismissed him by an order as if the parliament did not exist and the principle of parliamentary responsibility was of no consequence. The Governor-General might have had full justification for the action he took; but no one could claim that it conformed to democratic principles. Instances could be multiplied to prove that in many of the new countries, which enjoy the forms of democratic government, the spirit is often forgotten—or more simply not understood.

Democracy in fact is not merely a form of government; it is a complex of social, economic and political factors, affecting the relationship of the State to the individual, guaranteeing essential freedoms, personal liberty, freedom of expression, of organisation and of normal activities, etc. These may be denied even in countries which have all the paraphernalia of democratic government. Undoubtedly even these basic conceptions have to be defined in relation to the conditions of each country. Also ideas in regard to freedom, equality, etc., have undergone very considerable change during the last half a century. Equality can no longer be defined as a career open to talent or as equality of all before law. It necessarily involves an element of economic equality. So also the conception of the freedom of the individual; originally it meant no more than freedom from illegal arrest or, at the most, the right of the individual to pursue his own avocations without interference. Today in democratic countries it is recognised that the conception of freedom includes such ideas as the protection of the weak and the underprivileged against the more powerful sections of the community, the oppor-

## Political Structure

tunity to earn a decent living, etc. These changing conceptions are a part of the democratic way of life, and no country, however perfect its constitution, which does not seek to attain these objectives in terms of its own conditions, could be considered democratic.

To take an instance. The principle of equality so far as India is concerned should mean primarily the abolition of caste—an institution based essentially on a doctrine of inequality based on birth. Whether India is in fact a democracy or only so by the definition of its constitution is to be determined by the action that the government takes on this important question, and the people's reaction to it. Such action again is to be considered not merely in terms of legislation, but of social attitude, economic policies and political power. The new States which have accepted the political forms without interpreting democratic values in terms of their own life must, of necessity, therefore, give the impression of being imitative and artificial and may, in course of time, become a parody of popular government—a dictatorship or an oligarchy behind a façade of democratic forms. This is the major problem of democracy in new States, and nowhere except in India does there seem to be a serious effort to give meaning and substance to these conceptions.

We have noticed that intellectual dynamism in democracy is provided by co-operative thinking spread widely in groups and institutions throughout the nation. Equally, the working of a democracy more than any other form of government is dependent on voluntary associations of people and the willing and unpaid labour of educated classes. Party organisation has become an essential part of the machinery of democracy. A party in a democratic country is not merely a group of people united by self interest—a faction, as Burke called it, but a national organisation which mobilises political opinion for action

*Afro-Asian States*

along certain defined lines. When the nation is equated with the entire people, organisations for bringing the people into action in the political field become necessary. In fact, no democracy can work without organised parties providing a machinery for political action. The essential characteristic of a party in this sense is that it is a voluntary organisation functioning, broadly speaking, on the basis of voluntary, unpaid labour. No doubt party organisers are paid employees, but the functioning of a party depends not merely on organisers but on an army of unpaid workers from members of central committees at national headquarters to humble volunteers at meetings and rallies. Besides, this immense machinery, which has to arrange for national organisations, continuous discussions of programmes, campaigns for the popularisation of policies, has to be paid for by voluntary subscriptions. All this means the existence of personnel at all levels with sufficient interest and enthusiasm to devote themselves to public work and sufficient financial support from the public. In fact, democracy involves continuous and widespread interest in public affairs among a large group of the people.

Most of the new States which became independent after the Great War had inherited party organisations of one kind or another. In India the National Congress, originally built up as a movement for independence, had transformed itself into a great national party after 1936. In Pakistan the Muslim League, in Burma the Anti-Fascist People's League (AFPL), in Tunisia the Neo Dastur, and the Istiqlal in Morocco fulfilled, more or less, the same functions. But the development of parties has not necessarily been on democratic lines in many countries. The Wafd, in Egypt, for example, had no national organisation, though its influence with the people made it a great political force in its early days. In the fight for independence such an institu-

## Political Structure

tion provides, perhaps, an adequate machinery, but the working of democracy requires also, as we have noticed, the normal functioning of opposition parties, wedded to democratic methods. Recent events in Indonesia and the Lebanon have shown that this is not a development which can be taken for granted in the new States.

One other aspect of democracy—one of its basic assumptions—may also be briefly touched upon here. The subordination of all other powers to the elected representatives of the people, i.e. the sovereignty of parliament, is the underlying conception of democracy. It is, therefore, assumed that the armed forces owe a duty of absolute obedience to the civil authority represented by the cabinet. It requires no argument to prove that a democracy cannot function except on the basis of the obedience of the army to civil power. But from the time Cromwell walked into Parliament and asked that the bauble be taken away and sent the elected representatives of the people back to their homes, to General Massu calling for the resignation of a Prime Minister-designate, the history of democracy is strewn with instances of conflicts between parliamentary authority and military power. Bonaparte with his party of soldiers at the National Assembly, General Yuan Shih-kai dissolving the Chinese parliament, the terrorisation by the Japanese militarists of successive cabinets are but a few and random instances of the successful refusal of military authorities to obey the orders of Parliament. The new countries of Asia and Africa have produced many instances of this contradiction. One of the transient military dictators of Syria, Col. Shihakly, expounded to a distinguished visitor that the only true democratic force in Syria was the army and, therefore, it was but right on the basis of democratic principles that supreme authority should be vested in the army. The first action of the Military Council which took over power in Egypt was to dis-

## Afro-Asian States

solve all political parties. The latest example of this conflict is in Indonesia, where the authority of parliament is being defied by a group of young colonels, no doubt on the ground of defending democracy.

It is obvious that solely on the basis of democratic theory the subordination of the armed forces to parliamentary authority cannot be enforced. What, then, is the sanction which democracy has to prevent the divorce of military from civil authority? It is the prevalence of the democratic spirit in the people as a whole, together with a determination to defend democratic rights that ensures the subordination of the army to parliament. If democratic institutions are only formal, or have become discredited with the people, then the army becomes a rival centre of power. This is a danger which faces every democracy not only in Asia and Africa, but all over the world. In the new States of Asia and Africa the danger is all the greater as the principle of democratic obedience is unfamiliar and the acceptance of authority based on effective power is traditional.

# II

# The Problems of Administration

DEMOCRATIC government is primarily a question of political leadership. But political leadership is only one aspect of the activities of the State; the actual administration of government is carried out by a hierarchy of trained personnel. Parliaments and assemblies determine policies, educate and direct public opinion, even exercise control over the machinery of government, but the actual execution of policies has to be by the trained machinery of administration.

In Europe the organisation of administrative machinery is a comparatively recent phenomenon. The feudal society from which the modern State developed in Europe paid but little attention to administration, which developed generally as a part of the household of the king. As democracy in Europe had its origin in the struggle of the people against monarchical absolutism, there was a considerable prejudice till at least the eighteenth century against officialdom as representing royal power and as a threat to the rights of the people. Even in nineteenth century England, officialdom was hardly mentioned in discussing the political structure of the country, which it was held was parliamentary and democratic. For example, in Bagehot's celebrated book on the English Constitution there is hardly a mention of the permanent Civil Service. Equally, in Prof. A. V. Dicey's *Law of the Constitution*, written in the first years of the present century and for long considered a classic, the role of the Civil Services in the Constitution

*Afro-Asian States*

is not discussed at all. In America what used to be known as the 'spoils system' prevented, till quite recent times, the development of an effective administrative machinery. In fact it may be said that the development of efficient administrative services under a system of parliamentary democracy is quite a recent phenomenon in the West.

Today the position is very different. The change in the character of the State and the immense and continuing enlargement of its functions not only in political, but also in economic and social fields, have helped to change the balance between politics and administration. The change has been so remarkable that a leading political thinker in England has gone to the extent of describing the English political system as 'parliamentary bureaucracy'.

The course of evolution in the countries of Asia and North Africa was altogether different. They were from the earliest times administering States. In ancient Babylon, Egypt, India and China, government from the earliest times was based on administrative services. This was due to the fact, as Max Weber and, following him, Karl von Wittfogel, have pointed out, that the States of Asia and Africa were based on land revenue administration, which again depended, in most cases of high Asian civilisation, on the control of river water and/or other forms of irrigation, requiring a large army of officials to administer. In India a complete and elaborate system of bureaucratic administration existed at least as early as the fourth century B.C., as may be seen from the *Arthasastra* (or the Science of Polity) of Kautalya.

The countries of Asia had thus an administrative tradition, and during the colonial period of their history this system came to be developed further. By the very character of the foreign rule, government was non-democratic and not based on elective institutions. The essential functions of government were only the maintenance of law

## The Problems of Administration

and order and the collection of revenue, and these required large administrative services. In India, Pakistan, Ceylon, Burma, Indonesia and the Sudan, and the countries under French rule, the colonial governments had created an efficient administrative machinery.

But the machinery thus created had three major weaknesses. In the first place, its superior personnel everywhere came from the metropolitan countries. Even in India, where fifty per cent. of the superior Civil Services were Indian by the time of the transfer of power, all the key posts were in the hands of Europeans. In finance, in the Ministry of the Interior, in defence, railways, transport, etc., the most important posts were held by Englishmen. The withdrawal of this top layer in the Service created a vacuum which it was no easy task to fill. In Burma the position was even more difficult. There the percentage of Burmese in the superior services was much smaller. Even in the subordinate services a considerable percentage was Indian. Besides, three years of Japanese occupation had destroyed the *morale* of the services. In Indonesia, the superior personnel had been almost exclusively European and even after independence it became necessary for the new State to re-engage a considerable number of Dutchmen. The case of the Sudan was particularly interesting. The Sudanisation of the services, which was considered a necessary step towards independence as both the executive and judiciary were in the hands of British officials, presented very difficult problems which were solved only by securing the services of personnel from India, Pakistan and other friendly countries on short-term contracts. This was possible as the official language of administration at the higher level was English. In Cambodia, Laos, Tunisia and Morocco, where the official language is French, the recruitment had naturally to be from France.

The second weakness of the administrative system in-

## Afro-Asian States

herited from the colonial authorities lay in its limited character. Colonial governments had been primarily interested in upholding law and order and creating satisfactory conditions for trade and investment. They had to collect revenue, administer justice and carry on with minimum interference in the affairs of the people. The machinery they created was in most cases admirably suited to these purposes. But once a State achieves independence, it is faced with other problems of equal importance. It has to develop an independent economic policy, undertake development schemes of various kinds, embark on a programme of industrialisation, enter into commercial relations with other countries, manage its own currency and face numerous other problems of a similar kind, all of which require highly trained administrative personnel. The experience under colonial rule generally did not equip these countries for work of this nature. To create administrative and technical cadres capable of dealing with the complex issues of a modern government is to every new State a problem of the greatest importance.

The third weakness of the colonial administrative system was the tradition of bureaucratic independence. As there was no immediate parliamentary authority to which they were subject, they became everywhere an independent governing corporation. During the period of British rule the Indian Civil Service, for example, though technically controlled by the Secretary of State for India as the Minister responsible to the British parliament, was in effect the Government of India. A majority of the posts in the Indian Cabinet was held by members of the permanent service. They held the governorships of most of the provinces and all the portfolios in the Provincial Cabinets till 1921. In effect, therefore, the civil services had but little experience of working under a parliamentary system. It is necessary to remember that in the West it is

## The Problems of Administration

the parliamentary system that existed first and the civil services were created as instruments for carrying out the policies of parliament. The evolution in the new countries has been the reverse of this. The civil services were long established institutions with a strong *esprit de corps*, traditions of initiative and of direct contact with the people, but with a non-democratic approach of paternalism, described appropriately in Indian slang as 'Ma-Bapism' or of being father and mother. Democratic institutions have been superimposed on this political and administrative foundation. As we have already noted, the implications of democracy are not well understood even among those called on to work it. Nor is the doctrine of obedience in democracy recognised clearly enough in most of the new States as against the authority of officialdom to which they have so long been accustomed. Except where the leadership of the new States as in India and in Burma is in the hands of men who by their fight for freedom had established an unquestionable authority over the people and earned their confidence, the tendency in many States has been for effective power to shift into the hands of officials and for the State to become a bureaucracy behind a parliamentary façade.

These three weaknesses of the civil services inherited from colonial administration are important factors in shaping the future of the new States. It has also to be recognised that the Services have so far in many cases provided the steel frame within which the States have been able to function politically even in the limited manner they have done. But the basic problem is of adjusting the inherited civil services to the tasks which modern States have to undertake. The newly independent States have many problems to solve which caused no worry to the colonial administrations of the past. This means not merely an enormous extension in administrative services,

## Afro-Asian States

but the development of skills in administration which the experience under colonial government did not help to develop. The administrative services in India are said to have multiplied three-fold during the last ten years. This is due not merely to the operation of what is known as Parkinson's Law, or because of any difference in skills between British and Indian administrators but essentially due to the change in the character of the State. Referring to the immense growth of the civil services in England after the war, Lord Attlee remarked in reply to a question in Parliament that the increase in the number of civil servants was due to the fact that England had become a Welfare State, and consequently the State had to administer many more things than it had to before.

This is even more true of a country like India which, after achieving independence, embarked on large scale schemes of industrialisation under government control and took in hand programmes of village reconstruction, rehabilitation of refugees, immense projects of irrigation involving reclamation, and colonisation of new lands. All this requires new types of administrative skills. The great new industries under State control require a different type of administrative personnel. Large scale multi-purpose schemes involving irrigation, electricity, etc., require not merely highly trained engineers but administrative personnel of high ability and experience. The Community Projects and National Extension Services which are designed to bring about a rural revolution covering the whole country require skilled personnel at all levels, which can not merely draw up programmes but work in close co-operation with the people of the village. An army of village level workers trained in new methods and capable of working with the rural population is required if a nation-wide programme of village reconstruction is to be carried out. Side by side with this, if a comprehensive

## The Problems of Administration

industrial programme has to be undertaken by the State, apart from training a managerial service, the new State has also to organise all available technical skills and bring them into the service of the State. In fact, the new State has to create an immense administrative machinery capable of undertaking many different kinds of activities.

Even if it were merely a question of expanding the personnel of a general purposes civil service, it would have been no easy matter in many States, as at the time of their independence many of them did not command a sufficiently large class of people with requisite qualifications from which such a service could be recruited. In Indonesia, for example, the system of education introduced by the Dutch did not make provision for a broad based intelligentsia. The Sudan, as we saw, had to start on her career of independence by recruiting civil servants on a contractual basis from other countries. Saudi Arabia, Yemen and Libya have had to depend to a large extent on the more advanced Arab countries for some of their trained administrative personnel. But in India, Pakistan, Ceylon and to some extent in Burma, where a more liberal educational policy had been followed, the recruitment of personnel for general administrative purposes did not meet with insuperable difficulties. By increased direct recruitment through normal channels, accelerated promotion, by the constitution of new cadres, by selection from public life, these States have been able not merely to fill the gaps left by the withdrawal of European personnel in their services but to expand them to meet their new requirements. Nor could it be said that there has been a noticeable fall in the standard of general services.

But the problem was altogether different when it came to matters involving specialised skills. All these new countries suddenly found themselves faced with the problem of an enlarged economic administration. The period fol-

## Afro-Asian States

lowing the war was one of controlled international trade, of difficult, complicated and very sensitive currency problems, of restrictions, rationing and controls in internal economy, all of which required specially skilled handling. Also it became clear in the very first years of independence that the changed conditions in the world required a complete reorganisation of the economic life of the new States. Not only had they to emerge from the stage of colonial economy, which circumstances had forced on them, but to develop their industries, mineral production and otherwise establish an independent and balanced economy. In the new States, obviously, this could not be left to private enterprises, not because of any prejudice against individual initiative or private capitalism, but because in most of these countries private capitalism had not developed to the extent necessary for this purpose. Except in India and Pakistan there was no notable capitalist class that had come into existence which could take the lead in a large scheme of industrialisation. Also there was the time factor. The basic problem in these countries was to catch up with the advanced nations of the West. A new factor had also entered into the situation by the emergence of China as a Communist State with a policy of rapid industrialisation. India, especially, had to embark on a programme of planned development covering every field. This required not merely detailed planning, itself a matter requiring very wide range of high technical ability, but a machinery which had the training and the advanced skills necessary for the implementation of plans. A personnel of control was no less necessary than an army of trained technicians. But it is obvious that the managerial function, the work of supervision and control, could not be entrusted to the personnel of a general purposes service like the Indian Civil Service. The mandarinate, so to say, insisted mainly on judgment, honesty and efficiency.

## The Problems of Administration

It was assumed that with these three qualities a civil servant could be entrusted with superior control of any department. Under the British administration this principle was considered, more or less, axiomatic, so much so that such posts as the Director of Industries, Chairman of the Port Trust, were entrusted to civil servants. But something beyond these essential qualities of judgment, honesty and general competence is necessary when it comes to the control and management of industrial and economic institutions. If a steel plant has to be administered, or a machine tool factory managed, the active head of the organisation would require also a great deal of knowledge of the problems of the industry. Also the personnel in direct control of the various branches of industry will have to be technical men of high training. This is not a matter in which a country can depend entirely on outside help. The advanced countries and international organisations may make available a few experts at different levels, but the country concerned itself has to produce the main body of personnel, both administrative and technical. India today has a very considerable body of administrative personnel. She has also over 80,000 qualified engineers, but it has been calculated that by 1962 she would require no less than 300,000 engineers; that is she will have in effect to quadruple her personnel with necessary engineering skills.

In practically every one of the other new States, where industrial development has not progressed to the same extent as in India, the problem is even more difficult. This problem we shall discuss in greater detail when we examine the questions connected with education.

The relationship between administration and political control is also a problem of some significance which the new States are facing. It is generally held that the function of political leadership is to lay down policies and it is for

## Afro-Asian States

the civil services to administer them. This creates a conflict of authority which cannot be overlooked. In countries with long democratic tradition, a line of demarcation has, in practice, been worked out, and it functions fairly smoothly. But in the countries where parliamentary experience is new and bureaucratic tradition strong and well established, inevitably political leadership and administrative authority come into conflict. In theory the Minister is responsible to the sovereign parliament for the administration of his departments. In fact, especially with the immense growth of administrative authority, this responsibility can be no more than nominal. Much of the effective power must rest with the Civil Service. Where, as in most of the new States, democracy is only formal and political control, therefore, necessarily weak, the conflict does not come much to the surface as the real authority continues to rest in the hands of the Civil Service. But where democracy makes itself felt and parliament is effective, the doctrine that administration is the function or responsibility of the civil servants will be found to create conflicts of a serious character.

In India this problem came up for public discussion more than once. In a recent case it was the subject of a judicial enquiry in which a leading Minister of the Central Cabinet and one of the senior civil servants were concerned. Three points were involved in the case; the right of parliament not merely to elicit information but to control the actions of the Ministry in the administrative field; the total responsibility of the Minister to Parliament for the actions of his subordinates; and the demarcation of the authority between the Minister and the permanent civil servant. The finding of the tribunal, which was approved by parliament on all these three points, is highly significant. No one denied the absolute right of parliament to control the actions of the Ministry even in the adminis-

## The Problems of Administration

trative field. The total responsibility of the Minister-in-Charge, at least from the constitutional point of view, followed necessarily from this assumption; and this conclusion was further emphasised by the resignation of the Minister himself. No demarcation of authority between the Minister and the permanent civil servants was, however, considered possible, for if the Minister's responsibility was unqualified, clearly such authority as the civil servants exercised has to be on the basis of a practical working arrangement and not on any constitutional principle. In fact, of course, a very large measure of authority has to be vested in the permanent officials, and it is only on a well-understood principle of mutual loyalty that the system can function effectively. This is a lesson which has to be learned by painful experience in all new democracies, for the traditions, conventions and practices on which this co-operation rests only develop slowly and cannot be laid down by statutes or regulations.

One further aspect of the Civil Service in a modern State is important in relation to the new governments. The administrative services are by their very nature conservative as they have to view all questions from the point of view of practicability, of adjustment to existing situations and from the background of their own experience. It is this character of the Service that makes it one of the stabilising factors in a democratic government. This is all the more so when democracy is inexperienced and the electorate not politically trained enough to exercise effective control. Political leadership may and often does desire to introduce far reaching changes, which in themselves may be highly desirable. It is only the practical administrator who is in a position to work out the effects of such a policy, create the machinery for giving effect to it, and evaluate its reactions on other spheres of administration. Where the Civil Service is capable of

*Afro-Asian States*

handling such questions, not merely on the basis of precedent or past experience, but of the practical problems involved, they provide the essential factor of stability in a democracy.

It is obvious that the success or the failure of the régimes in the new States depends on the machinery of administration which they are able to create. Where such machineries have functioned with reasonable efficiency and adjusted themselves to the new conditions, the governments have also functioned satisfactorily. Where the administrative machinery has either cracked or there has been a failure to build up an adequate personnel in these services, the independence which the States achieved has remained nominal and there has been the haunting fear of chaos.

Briefly, the problems which the new States face in the administrative field may be summarised as follows. At the time of independence, the civil services which the States inherited were in every case weakened by the withdrawal of the superior personnel which of necessity came from the metropolitan country. Even in the countries where an effective Civil Service existed—though in an attenuated form—the changed purposes, motivations and enlarged activities of the State required an immense increase both in the supervisory and technical personnel which most of these States were unable to provide. Without such an expanding cadre of trained personnel the new States are in no position to bring about the essential changes in their economic and social structure, and must inevitably revert to a condition of backwardness and chaos. Where, as in most of the new States, the political structure is democratic, the problem is even more important, for a democracy cannot function without an administrative machinery of trained competence. In this sphere the loan of foreign experts and international technical assistance, though valuable, cannot basically alter the character

## The Problems of Administration

of the problem. The future of the new States, therefore, to a very large extent depends on the rapidity with which they are able to build up a competent, trained and honest administration, which will create the stability necessary to democratic governments and provide them with competent instruments of implementation.

# III

# The Problems of Economic Life

THE stern realities of economic life faced the new States immediately after their independence and made them realise that their political independence had but little value unless their economic independence was achieved along with it. Every State which emerged from a prolonged period of foreign rule found that its economy was in a measure 'colonial', that is, bound almost inextricably to the metropolitan country which administered it. Its currency was tied up with the currency of the metropolis. Its banking system was—except to some extent in India—dominated and in many cases monopolised by metropolitan banks. Its trade was, in the main, directed towards the mother country. Some of the major commercial products, like tea in India, tea and rubber in Ceylon, petroleum, sugar and rubber in Indonesia, to mention only a few examples, were predominantly in the hands of the colonising country. Even in the disposition of raw products the metropolitan countries had a dominant voice. Economically the new States were bound hand and foot, and if their political independence was to be given an economic substance, it was obvious that they had to devise policies and measures to which they had not given much thought previously.

Not only was such an action necessary from the point of view of economic freedom, but a more compelling necessity was to raise the living standards of the people. In every one of these countries the vast majority of people

## The Problems of Economic Life

lived on the margin of subsistence. Not only were living standards abnormally low, but the resources available to the State to provide the essential facilities in regard to education, public health, communication, etc., were meagre. Without exploiting the natural resources of the country and greatly increasing production, there was no possible future for these countries.

While it was, therefore, recognised everywhere that the creation of a balanced economy and a programme of industrial and other development were the first priorities, the difficulties which the States faced in these matters were also overwhelming. In the first place, no proper economic thinking had been developed in these countries. Economic thinking is related to economic structure and in the colonial countries such thinking as had developed was unreal as, in the main, it merely reflected the fashions of the metropolitan countries. In many countries the necessary technical skills did not exist; capital was in most cases lacking; proper surveys of natural resources had not been undertaken; and the communications system, railways and ports, even where they had been developed, had not been in terms of the needs of internal development.

One thing seemed clear. Without a system of comprehensive State planning these countries could not emerge out of their economic backwardness. The Russian experiment in planning had shown the way, and one of the major influences in nationalist thinking in the period before the war in India was the achievement of the successive five year plans in the Soviet Union which had converted the semi-colonial economy of Czarist Russia into one of the leading industrial nations of the world. In India in 1937, under the leadership of Nehru, a Planning Commission had been established to undertake exploratory work, a clear enough indication of how the mind of nationalist India was working. An added urgency was

## Afro-Asian States

given to this problem by the revolutionary changes in China. Though China's own industrial planning came a few years later, the Communist Government in China forced the problem of economic betterment on the new nationalist States of Asia. It became clear that unless radical changes were brought about in the economic conditions prevailing in these States and the living standards of the masses were greatly improved it would be difficult to avoid the danger of the Communist ideas spreading among the people. Planned economic development became, therefore, not a distant ideal but an immediate necessity.

But while every new State recognised the necessity for planned development, the problems that planning presented were discovered to be extremely complicated in themselves. It was easy to draw up plans on paper as the Abbé Sieyès used to draw up constitutions or as philosophers construct cosmological theories. But if such plans are to be put into practice, they have to be based on a survey of existing resources in every field; the availability of raw materials, the scope of power development, communications, the technical skills and other relative matters. It is not possible to plan on the basis of what does not exist. For example, almost everyone of the new countries has been planning to develop a steel industry, as steel has come to symbolise industrial progress. But it is obvious that in the countries which have no adequate supply of iron ore, no coal or other major sources of power and, above all, have not got even the beginnings of technical skill in this field, the planning of a steel industry is only a vain dream.

Political and economic immaturity is also reflected in the desire of each of these countries to become economically self-sufficient. Even in Europe many countries, even when they have the technical skills, do not think in terms of automobile industries and machine tool factories but

## The Problems of Economic Life

prefer to specialise in matters where they can achieve an international pre-eminence. Belgium, for example, which is a major producer of steel, has no automobile industry. And yet everywhere in Asia, planners seem to think in terms of autarchy.

The two basic problems governing industrial development in Asian countries are the lack of capital and the limited technical skills available to them. The economic backwardness of the State stands in the way of adequate capital formation in the country itself and without such capital no great industrial development can take place. To break through this vicious circle is the major problem of the new States. No doubt the Soviet Union, by enforcing extraordinary sacrifices on the people, was able not only to break through this vicious circle but reach the level of a self-developing economy. None of the new States we are considering has at its disposal the political machinery capable of such enforcement. A totalitarian State, with a determined policy, can carry out the most elaborate schemes, as it can mobilise the population and need not count the final cost. Also it is necessary to remember that during the period of Russia's first two Five Year Plans it was a buyers' market and it was not so difficult as it is today to find capital goods necessary for the first stage of industrial development. Every country which planned its industrialisation after the second World War had to look to the more developed countries for financial aid or investment, and for credit facilities for capital goods.

Foreign economic assistance to backward countries is a complicated problem which has numerous implications. The supply of large sums of money to countries which have no regular or fruitful channels of expenditure may itself become a dangerously unsettling factor. It may in such cases lead to the development of large vested interests creating conflicts within the country. The case of

## Afro-Asian States

Kuomintang China is well known. The very considerable sums which America advanced to that country between 1945 and 1948 served only the purpose of enriching the rich and creating a class of contractors and intermediaries which helped to widen the gulf between the people and the administration. In fact, foreign financial assistance in the absence of a competent administrative machinery and carefully worked out plans for expenditure may become more a source of public corruption than a help to industrialisation. The experience of the last ten years in many countries demonstrates this clearly.

Nor is this danger only when external capital takes the form of aid. The large sums of unearned income received by some of the new countries in the form of oil royalties have not, as is well known, led to any economic betterment of the people of the countries concerned, for there existed in these countries no organised machinery for utilising the funds for public benefit. Only recently in Iraq a programme has been worked out for industrial and social development on the basis of oil royalties. In Saudi Arabia, Iran and other oil-bearing countries, this immense source of income has not led to any economic development of a serious character and may indeed be said to have created contradictions in local societies which did not exist before.

The second problem is that of technical skills and scientific knowledge. Modern industry is based on scientific knowledge and technical skills which utilise that knowledge in the interests of production. It is obvious that no great progress in any field, least of all in industrial development, can be achieved on the basis of secondhand science. Without an adequate background of scientific knowledge which, even if it does not contribute to scientific thought, is able to assimilate and utilise the results of science, industrial development, however actively pursued, must lag

## The Problems of Economic Life

behind. This is a problem which we shall discuss later in greater detail.

Even at a lower level, that of creating and developing industries merely by following what has been done elsewhere, the problem of technical personnel and skilled workers is of primary importance. Most of the new countries are short in these two respects, and without considerable preliminary work devoted to the creation of the essential technical personnel, the development of such industries also would seem to present many difficulties.

India may be said to stand in a class apart in this matter. She had, during half a century preceding her independence, and more especially after the first World War, developed considerable industrial strength. Her first steel plant was established as early as 1908. The Tata Power Development Schemes had, even before the first Great War, shown the way of hydro-electric development. Her textile industry had become one of the most important in the world and, in cement and sugar, she had become practically self-sufficient. A powerful capitalist class had at all times been a notable feature of Indian society, and in the inter-war period it had begun to penetrate effectively into the British monopoly in organised banking and insurance. From the point of view of scientific knowledge and technical skills also, India had, during the first half of the twentieth century, achieved considerable progress.

Besides, her natural resources in all essential matters connected with industry were considerable. She had ample reserves of coal and iron ore. The possibilities of hydro-electric energy were not inconsiderable. Except in respect of oil and copper she is reasonably endowed by nature, and even in respect of oil there is a reason to believe that intensive prospecting may yield satisfactory results. Her system of communications was fairly well developed and

## Afro-Asian States

she had the advantage of a reasonably trained managerial class.

Her main difficulties were of two kinds. Indian agriculture was uneconomic and backward, and consequently, after the separation of Burma and the secession of the irrigated areas of the Punjab and Sind, she had to face at the very beginning of her independence a serious food-shortage. A feudal landlordism stood in the way of a progressive development of rural economy. The extreme poverty of the peasant and his conservatism were serious handicaps to any scheme of rapid increase in agricultural production. Secondly, India, because of its size, population and past history had to be organised on a federal basis which left the central government with inadequate powers on such matters as education, land reform, improvement of agriculture.

In the period immediately following her independence the problem of her backwardness in agriculture was emphasised by grave shortage of food grains amounting almost to a chronic famine. Valuable foreign exchange had to be diverted for procuring food from every available source. The political weakness of the federal structure made planning on these problems difficult, as the federal units, subjected to the pressure of local politics, failed to co-operate on some of the major issues like land reform. In spite of these handicaps, India was able successfully to launch her first Five Year Plan. But it is significant that in her first plan the emphasis was mainly on immense schemes of irrigation, rural reconstruction through community projects and national extension services, and industries directly contributing to better agriculture like fertiliser plants. The industrial sector of the first Five Year Plan was by no means unimportant: but it only laid the foundations of major advance. Private capital also played a notable part by developing such essential industries as

## The Problems of Economic Life

heavy chemicals, automobiles, textile and jute machinery and machine tools.

The success of the first Five Year Plan led India to embark on a much more ambitious scheme, with the declared object of developing the basic industries necessary for creating a self-developing economy. The difficulties facing a new country in re-organising its economy began to be increasingly felt at the end of the first year of the second plan. In relation to India the problem was mainly one of foreign exchange. She had planned to spend 8,800 million rupees (approximately 1,900 million dollars) on industrial development, and 13,000 million rupees (2,800 million dollars) on transport and communications. A considerable percentage of this money had to be devoted to the purchase of machinery outside India, to be paid for in foreign currency. The gap between India's earnings of foreign currency by export and her expenditure abroad was found to be too great. Foreign aid through loans from the International Bank, and from countries both in the West and in the Communist East as well as credit facilities had to be secured if the second Five Year Plan was not to founder. Fortunately India was able to negotiate such assistance and go forward with her plan, though some of her important projects had to be modified in certain respects. But the importance of India's economic effort was recognised by the more advanced countries, the American Senate going to the extent of specially underlining the importance of aiding India to work out her plan successfully. The projects for increasing India's steel production from 1.2 million tons to 5 million tons, the major schemes of irrigation and power development and the development of many basic industries are now going forward as a result of financial assistance and credit facilities provided by the major countries.

But India's case was a very special one. She was able

## Afro-Asian States

to mobilise her considerable internal finances, utilise the modern technical skills she had developed during the last half-century, make arrangements for the training of a vast and ever-increasing body of technicians and call into her service a corps of scientists. In fact, she was actually on the doorstep of a major industrial revolution, and the political stability which she was able to achieve within a short time enabled her to secure adequate external assistance and, at the same time, follow a consistent policy. The other countries of the Afro-Asian region did not possess these advantages. In most countries political stability could not yet be said to have been achieved, and except in Pakistan many of the other requirements of industrialisation did not also exist.

The transformation of the economic life of the new countries is not solely a problem of industrialisation. The vast majority of the populations of these countries lives in villages, in a state of extreme poverty, following a primitive agriculture. The creation of industries in urban areas in however progressive a manner could provide no solution for their poverty or, in the immediate future, help to raise their standard of living. Unless the economic development of the rural areas went on side by side with urban industrialisation, the result would unavoidably be to widen the gulf that already exists between urban and rural life in these countries: an industrial urban population receiving higher wages, possessing modern amenities and living a better life, with the rural population plunged in ignorance, poverty, and living on a margin of existence as in the past. This is by no means a new experience in the process of industrialisation. During the first half of the nineteenth century when the social effects of the industrial revolution in Europe became clear, many observers noted that in England, for example, 'two nations' had come into existence, one rich, progressive and living

## The Problems of Economic Life

a life of luxury, while the other was steeped in poverty.' The doctrine of class war which Karl Marx developed, though based on the gulf between the capitalists and the working classes in industrialised England, also emphasised the same point.

This problem of the existence of a highly industrialised section side by side with a poor and ignorant rural population is particularly important in these new countries. Its revolutionary potentialities could not also be overlooked. With Communists ready to exploit the conditions under the leadership of a dynamic urban proletariat which develops as a result of industrialisation, such a divorce between urban and rural development must unavoidably lead to a Communist revolution.

The transformation of rural economy is, however, a very difficult problem and has not been seriously attempted except in India and to a lesser extent in Pakistan. It involves an integrated development of village life, modern techniques, better methods of cultivation, the creation of small scale industries suited to the villages, modernisation of handicrafts, ensuring a general sense of prosperity and progress. The villagers everywhere are conservative in their social traditions, methods of production and in their community life. The introduction of new techniques into rural life creates special problems: and yet without such techniques, higher production, greater prosperity and better life are not possible. India has sought to solve this problem by a system of national extension services and community projects. These attempt to create a development unit of 80 to 100 villages, and provide it with a plan of development which would cover every aspect of life; better communications, provision of medical and educational facilities, introduction of small scale industries, better techniques in agriculture—in fact an integrated scheme of betterment based on local effort though with Government direction, advice and financial assistance. To bring all the five hundred and seventy thousand villages under a scheme of this nature is a herculean task involving not only heavy expenditure but the creation of an army of trained village-level workers who could create and canalise the enthusiasm of the village population. So far within the last eight years the Indian Government has been able to cover over 300,000 villages, and under the present scheme hopes to cover the entire area by 1962. Everywhere the scheme has not been equally successful, but everywhere it has generated new forces and brought the villager out of his old fashioned way of thinking.

One of the major handicaps which any scheme of village development has to face is the inadequate supply of electric power. Without electricity reaching the villages it is not possible to develop rural industries or create satisfactory conditions for better life. Rural electrification has progressed only in some advanced areas, and there village development has shown very satisfactory results. The total installed capacity at the end of the first Five Year Plan was only 3.4 million k.w. It is being expanded at the rate of about 20 per cent. a year. Obviously it will take some decades before electricity can be supplied to every village in India.

In other countries the problem has not been seriously considered. In Pakistan the Village Aid scheme has made some progress, and by fits and starts Egypt also has attempted a programme of village reconstruction. Otherwise, as a result of the lack of internal stability and a failure to recognise the urgency of the problem, the development of rural areas has generally been neglected.

Briefly it may be stated that the economic problems of the newly independent States fall under three categories.

(1) The creation of a balanced economy suited to the

## The Problems of Economic Life

conditions of each State in place of a colonial economy tied to the interests of the metropolis.

(2) The development of industries and the exploitation of natural resources in order to enable the new States to provide for a better life.

(3) The transformation of rural life and the modernisation of agriculture so that the peasants who constitute the vast majority of the people of these countries may come out of their age-long torpor and share in the prosperity of the nation.

All these aspects are equally important. The colonial economy developed during the period of their political subjection made these States dependent to a very large extent on the economies of metropolitan countries. The instability of this system was most noticeable in countries like Malaya (rubber and tin), Ceylon (tea and rubber), Indonesia (rubber and oil), Saudi Arabia, Iraq and Kuwait (oil), whose economic life was dependent on products necessary for the industries of the West. The development of a more balanced economy is, therefore, of primary importance to them.

Without the development of industries utilising to the fullest extent the raw materials and other resources available in the country such a balance could not obviously be created. This is not the only motivation of the schemes of industrialisation about which every new State dreams. No country can make substantive progress in the essential purpose of political freedom of providing a better material life for all, education, medical facilities, easy transportation and a much higher standard of living, in fact modernise the lives of their people, without adequate resources. In short, without increased production of wealth by the creation of industries, and the systematic exploitation of mineral and other endowments of nature, the resources necessary for the proper functioning of a modern pro-

## Afro-Asian States

gressive State would not be available and all ideas of national welfare and greatness would be but vain dreams.

The modernisation of agriculture and the transformation of rural life which have to proceed side by side with industrialisation are fundamentally important for the new States because the population pressure in these areas makes increased food production a matter of prime necessity. Also if the conditions of rural life continue as today, steeped in ignorance, poverty and bound to traditional ways, no amount of urban development would make the country progressive.

Only if this three-fold problem is successfully tackled will the new States reach the road which leads them to a self-sustaining economy. It is an obvious fact that a self-sustaining economy moves forward rapidly by its own dynamism and unless a State reaches that condition there will always be a danger of stagnation, or even falling back. This is the core of the economic problem of the new States. To reach that stage of self-sustaining economy is the ideal. Whether they achieve that end depends on many factors, the most important of which is a determination to sacrifice and work for a better future.

IV

# Education

ONE of the most important problems which faces the new States is that of education, both general and scientific. There are three special aspects of this question which arise out of the previous condition of dependence of these States. The first is that in everyone of these countries, excepting the Arab States, higher education is through foreign languages. Secondly, nowhere was there a system of national education reaching down to the people. Thirdly, education was mainly of a literary character.

It was in India that a large-scale educational system through a foreign European language was first organised and carried on for over a century. The system had some notable advantages in a country which had at the time no national unity and no dominant language. It created an educated class possessing a similarity of outlook; it helped to develop the Indian languages, and above all it gave a sense of unity to the country by providing it with a common language. But it also created a gulf between those educated in English and others educated in the traditional way or not educated at all.

Education even in secondary schools being through English, the extent to which it could penetrate was limited. After a hundred years of effort the number of people educated in English up to high school standard was less than 10 million. In Indonesia it has been stated that when the Dutch left there were only 14,000 persons with higher education in Dutch. In the Sudan the number was even smaller. There was only one college in Khartoum which taught up to University standards. In Morocco and Tunisia French education did not penetrate deeply.

Even where there were two systems of education, one based on the local languages and another through a foreign medium, education under the colonial system left the vast masses illiterate. For example, in India when the British left the percentage of literate people was only between 18 and 19. So the structure of the population from an educational point of view was the following: a very large illiterate base, a small percentage with education of a limited character in their own language, and a much smaller minority educated in English.

None of the colonial governments had ever thought in terms of mass education. So long ago as 1910 a very distinguished Indian leader, Gopal Krishna Gokhale, introduced a Bill in the Indian Legislature for making primary education free and compulsory, in the first place in urban areas. This very limited programme, it is interesting to remember, was resisted by the British authorities on the grounds of expenditure. During the last war the British Government in India, realising the absurdity of this position, set up a Commission under a very distinguished educationist, Dr. Sarjeant, to enquire into the problem and to draw up a scheme of national education which would eradicate illiteracy in India. His report contained many valuable suggestions but the programme he suggested would have made India fully literate only after 40 years!

The emphasis on the literary character of education undoubtedly helped to create a modern mind among the literate but it left most of these countries without an adequate supply of technicians and without a sufficient appreciation of modern scientific development.

The importance of education in a democracy is obvious. Democratic institutions can work successfully only where

## Education

there is a very considerable base of educated people. Taking the case of India, Central and Provincial Parliaments have a membership of over 3,500, and in a genuine democracy it would require at least double the number of candidates seeking election. If to this figure is added the number of members of other elected institutions like city corporations, municipalities, district boards and village bodies and numerous institutions like University Senates and advisory bodies to public institutions, the number of educated people necessary to run the democratic machinery of administration would run into hundreds of thousands. Again, the ever increasing civil services of government and of industrial administration, both public and private, apart from the large army of teachers for educational institutions, would mean an immense addition to the class of people of superior education and general competence.

An equally important problem is that of scientific and technical education. This requires separate consideration, in terms of the new industrial revolution which the world is witnessing and will, therefore, be discussed at some length later.

The nature of education in the newly independent countries is something to which not much thought has been given before. Generally speaking, in these countries the system of education was based on the ideas prevalent in Europe in the nineteenth century. In India, with a long tradition of humanistic studies, education provided no incentive for work. The mandarins of China, it is said, used to grow long nails to show their aversion to physical labour. In fact the educated man in Eastern countries may generally be said to have cultivated an attitude of looking down on manual labour. This *brahminical* type of education admirably suited the colonial governments as their main object in providing higher education was to

## Afro-Asian States

ensure a steady supply of white collar workers for government. Every man of college education looked forward to a clerical job in the Government—the career which was described by a cynic as that of 'writing with goosequills on foolscaps.' Mahatma Gandhi was the first man who emphasised the need for a change in the basic approach to education. From the beginning of the non-co-operation movement in 1920 he had experimented with educational problems and in 1936 he drew up a scheme, in collaboration with certain leading educationists, the object of which was to combine manual labour and training in arts and crafts with formal education. In one form or another the main principles of the Mahatma's educational system has been accepted by the Government of India. The Basic Education Schools which are being started all over the country are based mainly on his ideas.

Another aspect of the educational problem in the newly independent States is the necessity to create a new social ideal. Under the conditions of colonial life, education tended to have a conservative bias. The provision of an education which is conducive to mental unrest is not in the interests of a foreign government. The text books taught in schools and the attitude of mind sought to be created in these institutions tended naturally to depreciate national cultures and to emphasise the virtues of foreign rule. To create a moral *defaitism* among the people would seem to have been one of the purposes of colonial education. The new democracies have to think of education in other terms. In the first place, they have to eliminate those factors which create in the mind of the young a lack of self-confidence, or what is the same thing in a different form, an excessive assertion of national greatness as a reaction to the former official point of view. Further, a new social purpose has to be inculcated through education, for it is obvious that unless social organisation keeps pace

## Education

with industrial development the country as a whole will remain backward. Therefore, education for purpose of social activity and to develop a conception of service to the community has become a new objective of the State. Educating young men in the principles of social justice, of the welfare of the community and of service to the nation, in fact the creation of a new social conscience—which colonial administrations could not undertake—has become a function of the State.

The most difficult problem of all, which in a measure touches all these questions, is the problem of the language. As we have already noticed, in all the countries formerly under colonial administration, education was imparted through a foreign language, English in the countries formerly within the British Empire, Dutch in Indonesia, French in Indo-China, Morocco, Tunisia and, to a large extent, in the countries of the Middle East. This system, apart from limiting the area of education—as obviously a foreign language can only spread among the upper classes—prevented the development of a national system of education. A system of universal education is possible only in the language of the country itself. But this question of a foreign language raises other major problems. None of these languages—even Arabic and Persian—however well developed from the literary point of view—have so far a literature of scientific thinking, or even the necessary text books for teaching modern subjects. Therefore, if education in the new States has to be modern, and if it has to prepare the people for the scientific age, then obviously one or other of the great European languages has to be continued as a medium of higher education at least for a time. In India, for example, though Hindi and some of the other languages are highly developed from many points of view, higher scientific or social thinking has not yet begun to be reflected in any important degree in them.

## Afro-Asian States

It is rightly pointed out that two hundred years ago similar problems existed in regard to German and Russian. Even in the nineteenth century Russian was considered a backward language for scientific work. In Germany even so great a national hero as Frederick the Great preferred to write his anti-machiavel in French. If one goes further back one could see that Bacon—a master and one of the fathers of English prose—thought that English was too much of a vernacular at least for the purpose of scientific discussion and wrote his major work in Latin. In modern times Japan transformed (within a reasonably short time) her language to one capable of handling the most advanced modern subjects. No doubt Hindi, Persian, Arabic and all other languages of the new States could be transformed in the same way. But the difficulty is the time factor. A considerable period had to elapse from the time of Peter the Great, who introduced wholesale the scientific and political vocabulary from the West, to the emergence of Russian as a language capable of expressing the highest scientific thought. It took Japan a period of fifty years to transform Japanese into a modern language. But the march of events today is so fast that the new States could not afford to wait so long.

Every country in Asia and Africa that has become independent recently faces this problem of giving modern education through a national language. Every country desires to give education through its national language; and rightly so, for these great languages represent to them not only values of supreme importance, but are integrated with the national mind. If the people have to be integrally developed, education has to be through the mother tongue; equally, at the present time it is only through highly developed Western languages that these countries can keep up with the scientific, economic and social thought of modern times. Merely because we desire to be educated

## Education

through our own languages we cannot afford to neglect the study of the latest developments in science.

The question of eliminating illiteracy is one which faces every new nation. Of course, there is no integral connection between independence and literacy. Universal literacy is a very modern phenomenon and even in the countries of Western Europe during the days of their historic greatness, the majority was illiterate. Spain in the age of Cervantes; France in the age of Louis XIV, Corneille, Racine and Molière, and later during the period of Enlightenment, and England even up to the middle of the nineteenth century, were largely illiterate. What is important, if it is merely a question of the effective direction of the nation, is that there should be a large enough body of educated people from whom the leadership of the nation could be drawn. But in the circumstances of today, especially when the political structure is that of a democracy based on adult franchise and when economic advance requires skills at all levels, the benefits of education must penetrate to the whole nation. This creates for the new States two different problems; the first, of educating the adults who have passed the stage of formal school education, and secondly the education not only of the existing number but the provision of facilities for the new daily increasing population.

In a country like India, where only 25 per cent. of the population is literate, and political power is based on adult franchise, the provision of facilities for adult education is particularly important. It is not, of course, necessary that such education should be based on what used to be known as the three 'Rs', reading, writing and arithmetic. Mass communication methods, radio, cinema and television, have changed the character of adult education and have increased the possibilities of visual and auditional methods. What is obviously necessary in a demo-

## Afro-Asian States

cracy is an apparatus of judgment. In the past it was possible for the most part only through reading; consequently, adult education meant almost exclusively teaching people to read and write, thereby providing them with a key to knowledge. Today for adults the basic knowledge necessary for judgment can be given in an ever-widening circle through visual and auditional methods.

Educating the new generations presents even more difficult problems. In India the growth of population is to the tune of five millions a year. Educational facilities in the primary stages have, therefore, to be provided for an additional five millions annually, if the State desires to enforce compulsory primary education. A very considerable increase in secondary, university and technical education must also be provided for. Taking a ten year period, India will have to establish primary schools for 50 million additional children, and high schools, colleges and universities and technical institutions to absorb at least a portion of this increase. This is, of course, without taking into consideration the immense expansion of education necessary to meet the requirements of universal primary education of children who are now of school-going age, almost 55 per cent. of which are without such facilities. The human and financial resources to build up an educational system of this ever increasing size—school buildings, trained teachers, text books and aids to teaching—constitute almost an insuperable problem. Even in countries like the United States, this problem of the expansion of educational facilities to meet the annual increase of population is causing major difficulties. How much more complicated would it be the case in countries like India, Indonesia and Egypt, where the problem is complicated by the fact that not only has provision to be made for the new increases, but also for a large percentage of the existing population.

## Education

No less difficult is the problem of University education. The Sadler Commission on University Education in India, so long ago as the second decade of the twentieth century, pointed out that the demand of the middle classes in India for university education had become a revolutionary fact. Almost every year new Universities are being established in India, and after independence the number of universities has risen to thirty-eight; and yet India has not been able to meet this growing demand. There are colleges having as many as 4,000 students, with teaching work being carried on in three shifts as in a factory. Additional universities can no doubt be established, but the provision of administrative personnel, teachers, lecturers and professors of requisite qualification is no easy task.

The problem that faces every new State is whether it should concentrate on a high standard of education for a limited but large enough section of people and neglect for the time the problem of universal education, or attempt the double task of providing a minimum education for all and, simultaneously, also attempt to tackle the problem of higher education. It is obvious that progress in the political, administrative and economic fields depends on the State being able to draw upon a reasonably large class of highly educated and trained people. This is, therefore, the primary necessity for every new State. If the provision of personnel for essential services, for industrial development and scientific research is neglected, the progress of the State must inevitably be retarded, and the resources necessary for financing a great system of national education will not be available.

This problem had not been foreseen in the days of colonial administration. In fact, as we have noticed, it is the democratic system that has made the problem of universal education an urgent one. A democratic system based on adult franchise inevitably postulates universal educa-

## Afro-Asian States

tion. It creates an irresistible demand for education which the government is compelled by circumstances to accept as a first priority; and yet no State is able to realise it.

The intensity of the problem varies from country to country. In India the percentage of literacy is now over 25. In actual figures, it means that out of a population of 375 million, over 90 million, almost the combined population of France and the Federal German Republic, are literate, a large enough pool from which she could draw the necessary personnel, especially as institutions for higher education also exist side by side. But in many of the new countries the number is comparatively smaller and the facilities for higher education much less. This is, perhaps, the explanation why countries like India and Egypt have been, in spite of their own educational backwardness, able to assist other countries in this matter. Ethiopia has recruited no less than 1,000 teachers from India for expanding her educational system. In the same way Egypt has been a source of supply in countries like Libya, Saudi Arabia, Yemen and the Sheikhdoms of the Arabian coast.

Though there is a widespread realisation that the problem of education in the new States is one of exceptional significance it is also realised that there is only a limited field in which international assistance can be extended to these States for a basic solution of their problems. For over a century now, leading Western nations have taken considerable interest in the education of Asian and North African countries. Missionary institutions in India, the American and French Universities in Lebanon and similar institutions in Egypt have helped to create the *new literati* in these countries. But they touch only a fringe of the problem. They have naturally concentrated on higher education and in many countries their contribution has been notable in this field. But the vast field of primary educa-

## Education

tion they have had to leave untouched. Apart from the immensity of the problem, in Asian and Arab countries at least primary education had to be through local languages and neither the missionaries nor the foreign governments interested could, therefore, help in this matter.

Also, missionary and foreign educational activities suffered from two major handicaps. Unavoidably their tendency was to emphasise European cultural and religious values. Consequently, with the growth of nationalism, these institutions, valuable in themselves, came to be looked upon with suspicion. Even the American University at Beirut, which had at one time been considered a centre of national renaissance, came under attack. Also, after independence, most countries began to emphasise their national culture, and it has not been found easy to adjust these foreign institutions to the new temper of the people.

Secondly, as the predominant share of foreign educational effort in these countries was in the hands of missionaries, there was naturally a religious atmosphere in the colleges and a Christian bias to their teaching. Even in the period of colonial authority this was resented by members of other faiths who formed the vast majority of the population of these areas. With independence this became a definite handicap, limiting the usefulness of these institutions.

In the period that followed the second war, which also witnessed the independence of most of these countries, some effort has been made to provide international assistance in the sphere of education. It takes the form of a supply of experts, study of special problems through seminars, investigation through specialists, provision for fellowships, training of teachers, etc. This work has undoubtedly been valuable, but again the extent of its usefulness is dependent on the capacity of the States them-

*Afro-Asian States*

selves to deal with the whole problem in a comprehensive way.

Briefly, the new States face a tremendous and almost insoluble problem in the field of education. This falls into three categories. They have to provide for universal education to their people, in itself a question requiring a long term policy, immense resources and concentration of national effort. In most Western countries universal primary education was achieved over a long period. The new States cannot, however, do it in a leisurely manner but are compelled to solve the problem in as short a time as possible or fall back in the race for modernisation. Secondly, they have at the same time to provide for a comparatively wide system of higher education to enable them to handle their administrative, economic and political problems; and thirdly, if their independence is to have significance they must provide for technical skills and scientific education. This three-fold problem faces all the new States in varying degrees and their future as independent States depends on how successfully they solve this problem.

V

# Science in the New States

TILL the beginning of the eighteenth century the differences between the countries of Western Europe and the major Asian civilisations were not particularly marked. From the point of view of science, technology and industry, the countries of Asia were not backward in comparison with those of Europe. In fact, the major trading activity of European countries during this period was the purchase of manufactured goods and cotton textiles from India, silk from China, etc. At the end of the eighteenth century the differences between Asia and Europe became marked. The Industrial Revolution and the development of capitalist production enabled Europe, by giant strides, to leave Asian countries far behind. In the ninteenth century the Asian countries had become in every material respect backward by comparison.

What brought about the change was the great advance in technology on which the industrial revolution was built. But the technology itself was the result of the revolutionary advance in science which the seventeenth, eighteenth and nineteenth centuries witnessed. By the time that the Asian countries awoke to this basic fact they had lost their political freedom and were in no position to reverse the trend. This backwardness only increased with every advance in science and technology in the West. One single instance may be quoted to prove this. Up to the middle of the nineteenth century India was a major shipbuilding nation. The British authorities themselves had

## Afro-Asian States

many ships built in Indian dockyards; but once steel came to be the major material used in the construction of ships, Indian shipbuilding ceased to be of importance, as India did not possess a steel industry and was consequently backward in the technology of steel construction.

There was only one important exception to this general development in Asia. When, in the middle of the nineteenth century, Japan was opened to foreign intercourse, her leaders, who had watched with alarm the defeat of the Chinese in the war with Britain, realised that the new learning of the West had to be mastered if Japan was to preserve her independence. She modernised her education, took to the study of science and mastered the technology which had given new power to European nations. By a heroic effort she was able within a reasonable time to bridge the gulf between the advanced scientific nations and the backward nations of Asia.

In China, apart from the political subordination to which the country had been reduced, the change in the educational system came only early in the twentieth century. Soon after, a period of political chaos followed the establishment of the First Republic (1912) with the whole country divided up under war lords. It was only in 1927 that a substance of unity was achieved and the work of modernisation seriously taken in hand. In India, the British Government had shown no interest in scientific education. Essential technical studies were, no doubt, inaugurated, but opportunities for the study of higher sciences were not provided. It was only in 1905 that a great and far-seeing industrial magnate, Jamshedji Tata, established the Indian Institute of Science. The next quarter of a century witnessed considerable progress in Indian scientific work, which received general recognition by the award of the Nobel Prize for Physics to C. V. Raman and the elec-

## Science in the New States

tion of a number of Fellows to the Royal Society, the premier scientific body of Great Britain.

But apart from Japan, China and India there was not even the beginning of scientific work in Asian and African countries when the second World War ended. With the achievement of independence every country embarked on an economic policy meant to raise the standard of living and create an industrial basis for its life. Immediately the problem of scientific work and technology faced them. In every vital sphere the backwardness of scientific work and the shortage of trained technical personnel were seen to be major handicaps. Not only industry, but modernisation of agriculture itself requires high level scientific work in numerous matters like soil research. Nor could the exploration of natural resources be satisfactorily undertaken without advanced techniques and the utilisation of the most recent scientific knowledge. When it comes to industry, its dependence on science was found to be even more absolute. Every major industry today is undergoing continuous change as a result of the development of science. The production and utilisation of new materials, the exploitation of new sources of energy, automation, improvement in machinery, all these emphasise the integral relationship between modern industry and science.

Scientific development, in its turn, is to a large extent dependent also on industry. While it is true that research in pure science can be undertaken independently of industry, the development of such discoveries and their utilisation for the benefit of mankind can only be done where a considerable industrial basis exists. Even if a scientist in his laboratory has mastered the theory of breaking up the atom and has perfected a technical process for doing so, the production of atomic energy could only be undertaken by a society which has large financial resources and a very high industrial potential. It is almost a truism, therefore, to say that high scientific work is possible to a large extent only in a highly industrialised society.

Further, many aspects of modern research deal specially with the problems that arise in the working of industry. New techniques and new processes change the nature of industry and create problems for the scientists to solve. The advance in industry is based on continuous research.

Similar is the position with regard to technology. High level technology cannot be produced except in an industrially organised society. Obviously, naval or shipbuilding technology cannot be produced in Nepal or Afghanistan, neither of which has any interest in shipping. Nor would it be practicable to produce a corps of steel technologists in a country which has no steel industry. No doubt when a country newly starts an industry of this kind the technologists could be hired, but without a technical and industrial background in the country itself no such major industry can succeed.

It is this vicious circle which is the most important problem in the new States of Asia and Africa. They have, with the exceptions previously mentioned, shown no great interest in scientific development, as they have no large industrial background; equally, there is no large scale industrial development in these countries because they have few trained technicians and no scientific personnel. To break this vicious circle is the first problem of the new States.

The new revolutionary developments in science during the last half a century have made the problem even more complicated. In every sphere of science during the last half a century the advance has been such as has never happened before. The basis of thinking in natural science may be said to have been revolutionised. The way it has affected the material set-up of life during the last half-century is itself something no one could have foreseen. To

## Science in the New States

mention only a few which affect the life of almost every individual in civilised society: air travel bringing every part of the world near to each other, wireless, television, etc., giving enormous and unprecedented power to organised States, refrigeration and deep-freeze affecting vital changes in food supply, the fabrication of new materials which has increased the resources of nations, and antibiotic drugs which have eliminated many dreaded diseases; instances of this nature which have transformed the conditions of civilised life can be multiplied almost ad infinitum.

No one is yet able to foresee clearly how nuclear science is going to modify our lives and activities. As a source of energy it is obviously going to transform the organisation of industrial life. Most major countries are now engaged seriously in the work of producing nuclear energy. The recent experiments in England have taken the problem of energy one step further. It is an elementary fact in history that the character of industrial production undergoes revolutionary changes with every new advance in the sources of energy. The present dependence of industry on coal, oil or water power for the production of energy has to a great extent determined the location and development of industry. The countries which either did not possess these resources or control them, or did not develop the techniques for their extraction and utilisation, naturally became backward areas. A similar situation is facing the world today.

There is, however, one essential difference which deserves to be emphasised in this connection. Even in the days of coal and electric power the organisation of industry had become extremely complicated, demanding immense capital resources and an elaborate scientific background. The technology required for a successful and expanding industrial society demands very high scientific levels. As

## Afro-Asian States

it is, but few of the countries now considered backward have the resources or the scientific skills necessary to catch up with the existing differences. In the changed circumstances of the nuclear age, the gap between the backward States and the scientifically advanced countries will become practically unbridgeable. The technology required will be much higher and more complicated than at the present time. It has to be much more widespread than even some of the highly advanced countries find it possible to achieve. Scientific research itself in these new fields has become immensely expensive and beyond the resources of many of the medium-sized States of today. The consequence can only be that the scientifically advanced States, with fully organised scientific research and directed application of the results of such research to industry and conditions of life, will jump ahead of others by giant strides, rendering the gap between the two more unbridgeable than ever.

What is the future of the newly independent States in these circumstances? The question has to be considered from three different angles: (1) the creation of a scientific and technological background in these States sufficient at least to understand the results of new advances in science and their utilisation in their own States; (2) the creation of a corps of scientists who are able to carry on research in terms of the needs of their country; and (3) the political and economic implication of the new society. The first of these, which may be considered the essential primary step, is itself extremely difficult for most of the new States of Asia and Africa. In India it has been calculated that the successful implementation of the next Five Year Plan would require 300,000 fully qualified engineers. The existing number of such engineers is just under 80,000. The creation of an additional corps of 220,000 engineers in five years will strain the resources of any but the most developed countries of the world. But alongside with this, other and more specialised technicians for various types of heavy industries have also to be created. This is only one aspect. In every sphere a similar problem has to be faced, with the result that the scientific basis of education has to be overhauled so as to provide an immense pool from which such technicians could be drawn.

But the problem does not stop there. Without a much higher level of studies the latest results of scientific advance could not be appreciated or assimilated. This means a widespread organisation of scientific research in every conceivable field. The instance of India would show how complicated this question is. Since her independence the Government of India, realising that without an adequate scientific background covering the field of both pure and applied research there was no possibility of large scale industrialisation or of better utilisation of her natural resources, let alone taking her place amongst the advanced nations of the world, embarked on a policy of promoting higher scientific education and research. Her activity in this matter falls under three heads.

(1) The establishment of many higher institutions for research in pure science. In this category may be mentioned the National Chemical Laboratory, the National Physics Laboratory and the Tata Institute of Fundamental Research.

(2) The development of research institutions connected with the exploitation of national resources. The most important institutions in this category are the Central Fuel Research Institute, the Central Electro-Chemical Research Institute, the Central Metallurgical Laboratory, the Central Food Technological Research Institute, etc.

(3) Research institutions directly connected with the problems of industry. This covers a very large field with over 250 schemes of research in progress in over 60 centres

## Afro-Asian States

and includes such subjects as radio research and instrumentation technology, dye-stuffs and coal-tar products.

Without the training of high level technologists who could use the results of research, scientific advance by itself could not lead to immediate national progress. No single country among the new States is capable by itself of dealing with this problem without adequate outside assistance. Most of the new countries send young men to foreign countries for technological training. For example, India has over 7,000 students studying higher technology in different countries of Europe and America; Great Britain, Germany, France and USSR in Europe and in the United States and Canada in America. But it is obvious that such training, though unavoidable to start with, cannot solve the problem. From the beginning India realised this. She had undoubtedly the advantage of having a number of basic institutions but after independence the problem had to be considered anew as the technical skills required were of a much higher order because of the new programmes of large scale industrialisation. She, therefore, embarked on a policy of establishing regional institutes of higher technology, the first of which, planned on the model of a Massachusetts Institute of Technology, was established at Kharagpur in Bengal mainly as a post-graduate course of studies. A second institution has been set up in Bombay with the assistance of Soviet technicians; a third one is soon to be set up with German assistance, while the fourth will have the co-operation of the British. With these four institutes of superior post-graduate training in higher technology, and a steady flow of students to institutions in Europe and America, apart from training courses provided by major industrial concerns, it may be possible for India to face the problems of the scientific age.

In the field of nuclear research also the Indian Govern-

## Science in the New States

ment has been active. India's first atomic reactor, built by the Atomic Energy Department of the Indian Government, went into operation on August 4, 1956. It is being used for the training of personnel for atomic work and a considerably large body of atomic scientists have been trained in India and abroad for keeping India abreast in this important field.

This short survey of some features of the scientific activity which India is pursuing will give an idea of how much the new States have to undertake, not indeed to catch up with the more advanced countries but merely to be able to utilise the results of scientific research. It is obvious that but few countries among the new States are in a position to undertake a programme of this nature. No country now considered as backward, with the possible exception of Pakistan, has either the resources or the background necessary for such a programme. The fact is that scientific research has become immensely costly; further, it requires a scientific background which can only be built up as a result of a long range policy. Moreover, as already emphasised, science cannot develop in a vacuum. It requires an industrial basis. These factors make it impossible for many of the new States to embark seriously on a policy of scientific and technological research.

The difficulties of the problem were recognised from the beginning. The United Nations established a number of specialised agencies with the declared object of assisting the new States in dealing with problems of modernisation. The UNESCO, the FAO, the WHO and other bodies had as their objective the provision of technical assistance to these countries on the basis of international co-operation. They endeavoured to make the results of modern science available to the new States through the loan of experts and by special programmes. Some of these programmes are of very considerable importance, especially in the field

## Afro-Asian States

of preventive medicine and development of food resources. From many parts of Asia malaria has been practically eradicated. Important field research has been undertaken in dealing with wasting diseases. Schemes for improving animal husbandry, for more intensive cultivation of food crops, for popularising deep sea fishing, to mention but a few, are being worked with success. Also considerable assistance has been given to some countries in their schemes for the development of technical personnel.

Valuable as such assistance has been, it could not be said to have helped to solve the fundamental problem, that of making these nations scientifically minded and enabling them to keep pace with the march of science. External assistance must necessarily depend on the prevalence of skills up to certain levels in the country concerned. For instance, it is impossible for even the most advanced countries to provide technical assistance in the matter of atomic energy to countries in which knowledge of physical sciences has made no progress. Similarly, large scale medical research cannot be subsidised under technical assistance schemes when there is a lack of qualified doctors in the countries concerned. In fact it is obvious that the quality of technical assistance provided under international schemes must vary with the quality of technical skills that exist in a country.

It should be easy for a country like the USA, the USSR, Britain or France to transport bodily and establish and run in a backward country a highly advanced technical process, say a television system or a radio circuit; even to organise industries for this purpose in a country. But in the absence of native skills the result will not be an advancement of the country, but the effective loss of its political power. It will be remembered that in the nineteenth century among the recognised methods of imperialist penetration in backward countries were the construc-

## Science in the New States

tion of railways, the exploitation of oil and other mineral resources and similar schemes of technical development. In China at the end of the last century every imperialist nation competed for railway concessions while Iran and some of the South American republics had to pay a heavy political price for the exploitation of their oil resources. In fact, only countries like Afghanistan and Nepal, which deliberately excluded modern techniques or like Japan which made a serious effort to master such techniques, were able to maintain their complete independence.

A similar—and in many ways a more dangerous—situation faces the backward nations today. The techniques of the twentieth century are much more developed and much more difficult to master than those of the nineteenth. The changes in material life resulting from the scientific and technological revolutions are so far-reaching that no country can successfully keep them out. But their introduction would inevitably, in the case of backward States, mean a more or less absolute dependence on the more advanced nations.

Equally significant from this point of view is the rate of advance in scientific skills in the advanced societies. Scientific research is continuously transforming the nature of industry, its structure, the quality of its products, with society reacting to it in its own organisation and life. As this is a continuing process, the States which start far behind find the distance between the more advanced societies and themselves increasing as every day passes. It is true that in the progress of civilisation one has not got to go through every stage, but can benefit by the experience of others. Scientists in backward countries have not, for example, to re-discover the quantum theory or the principle of relativity or the process of nuclear fission. They can step straight into the new world, but without an adequate background they are in no position to utilise it;

*Afro-Asian States*

and by the time the more backward countries reach that stage, further and even more revolutionary advances would have left them behind.

The fact is, as we have emphasised before, no country can build up a modern society on the basis of secondhand science. In order to take advantage of the progress of science anywhere, a country must have a corps of scientists who are capable of exploiting and assimilating the results of the latest research. Most of the 'new' countries in Asia and Africa are in no position to do this. The transformation of their educational system for this purpose is itself a difficult process. Also, as we have noticed, scientific work cannot progress in vacuum, that is without a background of modern industry, which in its turn is dependent on a high level of technology.

Viewed generally the revolution in science which the last few years have witnessed faces the newly independent nations with many major problems. A recent conference held at Bangkok under the auspices of the United Nations to study this question in relation to the States of South-East Asia, that is the countries of East and South Asia outside China, India and Japan, noted with regret that there was but little interest in scientific development in these countries. The position in the countries of the Middle East and Africa is also not different. They are, broadly speaking, spectators in this fast changing scientific world; and the kind of assistance which international organisations offer them does not help to take them out of the non-scientific rut into which they have fallen. Briefly it may be stated, therefore, that the world is on the doorstep of a great transformation which will make the gap between the scientifically advanced and the scientifically backward nations deeper and wider; making the latter more than ever dependent for all essential things on the more powerful nations.

# VI

# The Social Problems of the New States

ONE of the major problems which all the States which have recently achieved their independence have to face is the re-organisation of their social structure to conform to the political, economic and moral ideas of modern life. Society in these States, most of which were formerly under foreign rule, had remained wedded to traditional forms mainly for two reasons. In the first place, the metropolitan governments in charge of administration generally followed a policy of neutrality in regard to social matters in the colonies and, secondly, as was but natural, the subordinate societies felt that their integrity was tied up with the traditions and customs of the past and held fast to them even when they disapproved of them. Consequently, at the time of their independence most of the new States found that the political ideas which they had championed and accepted as suitable to their newly found independence could not easily be reconciled with the social structure they had inherited.

It should be remembered that the traditional character of European society underwent radical changes only after the French Revolution. It was only after the revolutionaries had pulled down the structure of the *Ancien Régime* that status ceased to be the governing factor of social organisation, that equality began to be accepted as the basis of political life, that the economic rights of women came to be recognised and the right of the individual to freedom was guaranteed and upheld. Neither did these

## Afro-Asian States

and other features of free society come to be accepted all at once. It was as a result of nearly a century of legislation that the present structure of free society came to be accepted in Europe. At the beginning of the nineteenth century women had practically no right to property in England. It was only in the period following the first Great War that women were given equality of political rights. Similarly, it would be seen that most of the legislative measures which gave shape to the changed ideas of social life were the result of nineteenth century thinking.

Society is organised everywhere—even in the most advanced countries—on the basis of tradition and custom as continuously modified by law. Whether that tradition is called common law, *adat* or custom, it represents a social tradition. Even where it is based on some ancient code, as the Law of Islam, or the codes of the Hindus or Roman Dutch law, these represent earlier traditions which have been codified. In that sense all society has a traditional base. What differentiates a purely traditional order from the free society of today is the continuous modification of tradition through legislation to meet the changing ideas of social relationship.

During the crucial years of the nineteenth century and the first half of the twentieth century, when Western societies transformed themselves, because of the economic and political revolution of the time, the societies of Asia had already passed under foreign control and were not free to adjust their own social relationships. An autocratic foreign rule normally wants to let well alone the social structure of the subject peoples. In India, during the first half of the nineteenth century, some elementary attempts at social changes were made; but the experience of the Great Rebellion (1857-58), one of the causes of which was the widespread fear that the British Government intended to interfere with social habits of the people, led to the

## The Social Problems of the New States

proclamation of a policy of neutrality in social and religious matters. The result of this legislative inactivity in respect of social matters for a period of ninety years was that, while public feeling in respect of social customs and traditions changed rapidly and radically, institutionally they could not be changed. The most remarkable instances of this widening gap between custom and social conscience in the case of India related to the treatment of untouchables, and traditional laws in respect of marriage. For decades Hindu opinion was protesting against the practice of untouchability, or the social custom which segregated certain castes and denied them normal civil rights. But the religious and social neutrality of the British Government stood in the way of effective legislation to give effect to this most necessary reform. Again, Hindu marriage laws differed widely all over India. Under the orthodox systems no divorce was permitted; nor could widows remarry. Besides, there were also caste restrictions in respect of marriage. Public opinion for many decades had been clamouring for change, but the policy of non-interference in the religious and social customs of the people stood in the way of legislation.

These instances should prove how, under a system of colonial rule, the adjustments of customs, traditions and laws to the requirements of modern life was difficult if not impossible. Consequently, when the new States of Asia achieved their independence, one of the fundamental problems they had to face was that of modernising their societies. The question they had to decide was primarily what kind of society they visualised as providing them with opportunities for a better life. That problem was not an easy one. It is not, as many people in the West think, a problem of changing the social conditions in these countries to approximate to those of the West. There are many characteristics of Western societies which the new States

## Afro-Asian States

consider as unsuitable to their conditions; for example, the weakening of family ties. There are others which are the result of a different type of economic development. The problem for the new States, therefore, is to find a social ideal which will combine those aspects of their own inherited traditions which appear valuable to them with the new urges of our time.

Each State has to deal with this problem in its own special way, but change it must if it is to uphold its freedom and provide a new life for its people. It is unnecessary to emphasise that independence does not by itself mean social progress. But where the newly independent country has opted for a democratic way of life, social changes become inevitable as the normal values of traditional society conflict with democratic values. Equality, individual freedom, equal status for women, protection of the less advanced sections of society and similar conceptions are essential to a democratic way of life, and these are not always provided for in traditional societies. Where the newly independent States have opted for a traditional form of government, e.g. a monarchy as in Libya, or in Saudi Arabia, the situation is necessarily different as the social urges are not the same, and the demand for changes will consequently be weaker.

It may appear to a superficial observer that a traditional form of governmental institution would contribute more to stability and to the preservation of social order than a political system which postulates radical changes in established order. On closer examination, however, it would seem that this is not so. The demand for social justice, economic betterment, political rights, education and other facilities for individual development has become universal and no traditional structure, however medieval, however sanctified by time or tradition, can resist these claims. Everywhere the people are awake and demand

## The Social Problems of the New States

changes, and consequently, political institutions like autocratic monarchies and dictatorships are themselves sources of instability and unrest.

Where, as in most of the newly independent States, the people have opted for a democratic form of government, they have also opted for radical changes in their inherited traditions, customs and laws which stand in the way of democratic progress. The Constitution of India declares in its preamble:

'We, the people of India, having solemnly resolved to constitute India into a Sovereign Democratic Republic and to secure to all its citizens:

    Justice, social, economic and political;
    Liberty of thought, expression, belief, faith and worship;
    Equality of status and of opportunity;
        and to promote among them all
    Fraternity assuring the dignity of the individual and the unity of the Nation;

In our Constituent Assembly this twenty-sixth day of November, 1949, do hereby adopt, enact and give to ourselves this Constitution.'

The three principles enunciated in this formulation have been further spelt out in a declaration of Fundamental Rights, which have the force of law, and a statement of the directives of State policy incorporated in the Constitution. These, taken together, constitute the political, social and economic principles on which the new Government of India is based. Of these, tolerance of religious beliefs and freedom to propagate them are part of the tradition of Indian society. At no time in recorded history was the Indian State based on the identification of any religion with the State. Equally it may be considered that there is nothing in the social and political tradition of India which goes against the conception of individual freedom. But

## Afro-Asian States

when it comes to the conception of social justice, it would be clear that the system of caste is directly opposed to it. The doctrine of economic justice is equally new—as indeed it was in Europe also over half a century ago. But there is a basic difference between the two. There is nothing *against* the doctrine of economic justice in the social traditions of the past, except that it is a new conception. So far as social justice is concerned, it is not only a new conception, but something contrary to the ideas which had been accepted as axiomatic. The ideas of caste and feudalism are based on inequality of status. In this case free society involves a definite break with the past.

The basic question in the transition from a traditional order to a free society is the relationship of social institutions with religious beliefs. *Ex hypothesi*, religious beliefs are immutable, though by interpretation they also get adjusted. But such changes and adjustments are necessarily slow and are generally covered up by forms of tradition. Where social institutions, especially law and custom, have the sanction of religion and are considered a part of religious life, there is an inevitable conflict between them and the changing nature of free society. In most traditional orders, laws and social institutions are held to have the sanction of religion. For long it was considered that the traditional institutions of the Hindus like caste, early marriage, prohibition of widow re-marriage, were inseparable from the Hindu religion. As the Indian State systems in the past did not claim legislative authority in these spheres, such a view was generally accepted in the West and during the period of British rule emphasised by the conservative elements in Indian society. It is only after independence that this doctrine was unequivocally rejected and the social structure of Hinduism separated from its religious principles.

In Islam the position is different. The social structure

## The Social Problems of the New States

of the Moslem world is held to be a part of Islam as it is based on the Koran and the Sharia. As law and social institutions are so intermixed with religion, the problem of their relationship with the conceptions of free society becomes much more difficult. The principle of democratic equality, however, is a basic conception in Islam and consequently in this matter there is no conflict. But the laws of Islamic society are not, generally speaking, so easily susceptible of change. Revolutionary thinkers and political leaders like Kemal Ataturk have, no doubt, been able to separate religion from society, but his example has not been followed in other Muslim countries. There have been, no doubt, serious attempts to liberalise social thought in Islam, notably the movement for liberalisation associated with Sheikh Mahommed Abduh in Egypt and with the Indian Moslem leader Dr Mahommed Iqbal. But in both cases, after a short period of influence among Western educated intellectuals, the forces of tradition asserted themselves, in Egypt through the Ikwan ul Mussalmeen (Islamic Brotherhood) and in India-Pakistan through the Ahrar Movement. In both cases the emphasis has been on the integral relation of Islam with law and society. It should also be remembered that both these movements of liberalisation originated when Moslems in Egypt and India were under foreign domination and subjected to foreign intellectual influence. With independence, the hold of religion on society has gained rather than weakened.

One aspect of traditional society which shows evident signs of breaking down everywhere is the isolation and consequent autonomy of villages. This is due in part to the influence of free society, industrialisation, urbanisation and similar factors, and in part to the new conception of the State and government. In traditional societies the conception of government was limited to the maintenance of law and order, the collection of revenue and defence

## Afro-Asian States

from external foes. The change that came over Europe at the end of the nineteenth century of the State being conceived as the complex of all national activity and of having the duty of directing economic development, of ensuring the welfare of all, especially of the less privileged sections of the community, of looking after the health and education of all, had become equally a part of the new conception of the State in Asia. Even where the machinery did not actually exist for such comprehensive activities, the authority of the State began to penetrate into spheres where formerly no administration ever took direct interest. In the case of States like India, Pakistan and Ceylon, which had inherited a competent administrative system spread over the whole territory, the change in the conception of the State had immediate effects. The Community Projects and National Extension Services in India and the Village Aid Project in Pakistan are instances of this large scale penetration of national activities into the villages and breaking down their traditional isolation and bringing them into line with the general development of the country.

Significant also is the influence of mass communication media, like the radio and the cinema. The extension of radio service to the villages breaks down the cultural isolation of the rural areas. Though the limited extension of electricity to the villages has restricted the effects of radio, it is a growing factor in every country. The popularity of the motion picture, on the other hand, with the rural public and the change it has helped to bring about have been most noticeable during the last three decades. This is especially true of countries like India, Pakistan and Egypt which have large scale cinema industries dealing with social and economic conditions of the area. The influence of the cinema in bringing the outside world to the villages is something which cannot be over-estimated.

## The Social Problems of the New States

The effect of industrialisation on the breakdown of the village is two-fold. In countries like India and Pakistan industrial labour is mainly recruited from the villages. This labour force does not, as in European countries, cut itself away from the village. There is a continuous interflow, superfluous labour going back to the villages and new recruits continuously arriving from the villages. This two-way traffic, which is a significant aspect of life in India and Pakistan, has had the effect of introducing new ideas in villages and changing traditional village relationships. A portion of the earnings of the labourers in the cities reach the villages for the maintenance of families and relations, contributing to a change in the standard of life in the villages.

Another reason for the steady breakdown of village isolation on which the traditional society was based is the development of motor communication. The internal combustion engine may be said to have abolished the isolation of the villages. It is the distance between villages and between villages and market towns that was the basis of the isolation of the village and its traditionally self-contained economy. With the development of communications and of motor services, the villages are no longer isolated; nor is village production any longer determined by local consumption. The vegetables produced in the villages find their way to the market towns. The requirements of the villages are no longer made by village craftsmen, but bought from the market. This penetration of industrial goods into the villages is the most significant evidence of the breakdown of traditional society.

In one respect especially the influence of the cinema in undermining one of the basic aspects of traditional society needs to be emphasised; that is in relation to family and marriage. The traditional society everywhere is based on an authoritarian family, that is the authority of the parents

## Afro-Asian States

over the children. The tradition of the cinema has been an emphasis on youth, on romantic love and freedom of the younger generation. The traditional ethic of obedience to elders and of acceptance of paternal decisions in respect of marriage are held up, if not to ridicule, at least as reactionary. The influence of this continuous propaganda, especially as it touches the subconscious feelings of the young, has been remarkable in transforming family relationship in traditional societies.

The traditional society everywhere has been based on extended family relationships. The joint family in India was in many ways a unique institution. It involved joint ownership of property, common responsibilities, a strong group loyalty not only to the members of one's own family but to those related to it. In a traditional society its advantages were considerable. It provided a primitive system of social insurance, looked after the aged and the infirm, and provided the individual with a sense of 'belonging', giving him moral support and standing. The family, with its related groups, was a small community. It involved also a pooling of resources, which was of considerable importance in the case of trading communities. Elsewhere, in China and in the Moslem countries, the extended family was equally a feature of social consequence.

The political, legal and economic institutions which developed as a result of Western contacts first undermined and then broke down the joint family. Family loyalty came to be discredited in a society where the State claimed exclusive loyalty to itself. Democracy postulated the individual and not the family. Political conflicts separated generations; the younger groups normally holding more radical views which could not be easily adjusted with the authority of the elders. This was especially so in the first half of the twentieth century, which was broadly a period of political struggle. In China and in India the conflict

## The Social Problems of the New States

was especially noticeable. Lin Yu Tang's novel *A Moment in Peking* is a most interesting picture of this breakdown of family loyalties and relationships, which within a period of fifty years revolutionised the traditional family in China based on Confucian doctrines. In India the process was equally rapid as a result of the Gandhian movement. Everywhere among the middle classes the family was split in loyalty, the call of nationalism undermining the authority of the elders, who, broadly speaking, held to conservative views. Brahmin young men working among untouchables, defying caste and restrictions with regard to 'inter-dining', etc., sons of high officials non-co-operating with government, women breaking the rules of seclusion and going into public work and courting jails, these did more to undermine the joint family than the theory of individual freedom taught in schools and colleges.

Economic tendencies hastened the progress. The joint family was basically a system of holding land or of carrying on business. Land legislation and the system of taxation made joint holding of property uneconomic. The development of joint stock companies as a major factor in trade and industrial development reduced the importance of joint family firms which had been the norm in the past. In urban and official society the limited family of husband, wife and their minor children replaced the joint family.

This growing individualism has had far reaching results on the position of women in society. In the joint family the position of women was naturally one of dependence. The younger women were subject to the control of the elders, the head of the family, and consequently women had but little opportunity of developing their own personality. The limited individual family gave women, for the first time, effective freedom, both at home and outside.

## Afro-Asian States

The new woman was the mistress in her own house and had a certain amount of financial independence. She had for the first time opportunities of developing her own personality and of devoting her leisure to normal public activities. With the spread of education and with opportunities for work, the middle class women in oriental societies began to play a part in national activities. A significant factor in the life of the new States has been the political and social work of women. Everywhere in China, Indonesia, Burma, India, Ceylon, Egypt, etc., independence has meant the emancipation of women and their active participation in national life.

The attitude of traditional societies to women was one of protection; of safeguarding them from contact with the world. The family was a citadel created around women, and whereas among the economically under-privileged classes they had to work, the ambition of self-respecting men was to save women from that humiliation. This attitude of protection has to a large extent been replaced in 'individual families' by one of freedom and co-operation, which does not confine women to the kitchen and the nursery but facilitates the development of their own interests.

But it has to be emphasised that this breakdown of the traditional structure is not necessarily connected with the development of free society. Neither the change in the character of the State, nor the utilisation of mass media, has any direct relationship with free society. They are in fact in greater evidence in Communist societies. So far as industrialisation, urbanisation, development of communications and other features which help to break down the isolation of villages and undermine the traditional structure of rural life are concerned, they are common both to free Society and to Communist states. The question, therefore, is what the effect of such a breakdown is

## The Social Problems of the New States

on democracy, public liberty and other aspects of free society.

The immediate effect of this breakdown on new societies is a state of social instability. The rise of new classes, the growth of administrative, clerical, professional and commercial classes, the development of politically conscious working classes, the effects of adult franchise, transferring considerable political power to groups which in the past were under-privileged and continue to be economically backward, all these add up to a state of socialism balance. In place of a general static society there is today in the new States a society where new classes are clamouring for change and the traditional leadership in society is being displaced.

Nor can it be postulated that the breakdown of the traditional system will lead to the development of a middle class, conscious of its responsibility and committed to a programme of progressive development. In the new free societies the urge is for rapid industrialisation, without which it is felt that they cannot achieve economic progress and provide a better life to the people as a whole. The economic and other sacrifices necessary for such a programme of industrialisation must inevitably fall on the middle classes, where they exist, or will effectively prevent the rise of a middle class where they do not exist. The efforts of the new States to jump straight from a traditional society into a modern industrial society must, therefore, mean the elimination of the middle stage through which the European States progressed to their present prosperity. From the traditional society, either one passes to a practically classless society where the State controls all economic life, or it is held up in the course of its progress because of the lack of resources.

If economic development need not necessarily transform the traditional forms of organisation into a free

## Afro-Asian States

society, it is obvious that a free society based on liberal political traditions must inevitably lead to a breakdown of the traditional structure. The functioning of democracy, especially if it is based on adult franchise, must, at least to some extent, transfer political power from the upper and middle classes to the less-privileged sections of society. The upper and middle classes can, no doubt, maintain their influence and power as a result of superior education and skills, but only by identifying themselves with classes from which they were isolated before. Also, opportunities for employment, education and political rights combine to give women a new view of themselves which in turn undermines the assumption of traditional society.

The authority of religion in a free society is also a subject of great importance in its relation to tradition. One of the essential assumptions of a free society is freedom of religious belief. The consequence of this freedom and the non-interference of the State in religious matters is the weakening of the authority of churches and the sanctions of priesthood. One of the main props of traditional societies was the sanction that religion exercised. Everywhere this could be seen as a major fact. In India almost everything was alleged to be concerned with religious beliefs. Once religious freedom becomes a factor in national life, traditional beliefs, customs and social organisations come to be questioned, and it becomes impossible to enforce the *tabus* which had previously been freely accepted. Except where such customs had become parts of law, these were increasingly overlooked. The fight against such customs leads directly to the reform of religion. It is significant that every movement for religious reform in free society has been against traditionalism. The breakdown of religious *tabus*, priestly influence and of social practices having a religious sanction has been the noticeable characteristic of the establishment of liberal

## The Social Problems of the New States

political institutions on a traditional society. Even in Islamic societies, there has been a notable trend against such institutions as polygamy, seclusion of women and similar customs. The purifying of religion and the revival of the great religions of the East have gone side by side with the development of liberal ideas in society.

In conclusion, the effect of the liberal ideas of the free society on the traditional order may also be viewed in terms of nationalism. In most countries under foreign rule, the traditional order resisted every kind of change as a defensive measure against the encroachments of a foreign culture. It was a negative nationalism which emphasised what was known as the genius of the community as its special hall-mark of culture. But with independence this nationalist approach to the traditional order lost much of its force. What nationalism was concerned with, after independence had been achieved, was to reorganise its social structure in order to make it effective, to give a greater sense of community and to bring its laws and customs in conformity with its ideas of progress. Conservatism ceased to be equated with nationalism, and the traditional order began to be examined from the point of usefulness and its conformity with the desire for progress.

---

In the foregoing pages I have attempted to discuss some of the major problems that face the newly independent countries of Asia and Africa. Their problems, as I have tried to emphasise, arise mainly from the fact that for over a hundred years which witnessed revolutionary changes in the economic, political and scientific life of the Western world, these countries were under foreign rule. Primarily it had two results; it changed the course of their evolution, leaving them at the time of their independence in a state of political and social uncertainty,

*Afro-Asian States*

with their own traditions undermined if not altogether destroyed, and with the new ideas imported from the West only imperfectly understood and partially assimilated. Secondly, it had deflected the course of their economic development, subjecting them in effect to a colonial system of economy. They stepped out of their dependence in a state of economic backwardness, insufficiently equipped to deal with the tremendous problems which faced them.

Also, the world into which they emerged as independent nations was in itself undergoing revolutionary changes in every sphere. It was dominated by the fears and complexes no less than by the hopes and expectations which the new and startling scientific discoveries created for the world. Suddenly, at the very beginning of their life as independent nations, they were faced with problems which were causing concern even to the most advanced nations of the world. The old world relationships had broken down as a result of atomic power. Industrial organisation and production were undergoing a revolutionary change. In fact, it was altogether a new world to share in which most of them were not adequately prepared. Naturally, the problems they had to struggle against became infinitely more difficult.

To confess this patent fact is not to be pessimistic about the future of these States. Difficulties exist to be surmounted by the will, persistence and energy of man. In varying degrees all these countries are facing up to these problems. To what extent they will succeed depends on many factors, not the least of which are the vision of their leaders, the response of the general public, the new dynamism which political independence has given to the people, and the assistance and sympathy of more advanced nations.

# INDEX

Abduh, Sheikh Mahommed, 87.
ADMINISTRATION (see also Civil Service).
  under Colonial Rule, 32-5.
  Evolution in Europe, 31-2.
  Evolution in Asia, 32.
  Political Control, 39-41.
Adnam Bey, 21.
Afghanistan, 79.
Agriculture, 36, 50, 52-4, 56, 71, 78.
Ahrar Movement, 87.
Albania, 15-16.
Anti-Fascist People's League (Burma), 28.
Ataturk, Kemal, 16, 87.
Atomic Energy (see also Nuclear Science), 71, 73.
Attlee, Lord, 36.
Austria, 15, 16.

Babylon, Ancient, 32.
Bacon, Francis, 62.
Bagehot, 31.
Bangkok, 80.
Banking, 44, 49.
Basic Education Schools (India), 60.
Beirut, American University at, 67.
Belgium, 15, 47.
Bombay, 76.
Bombay University, 23.
BRITAIN.
  Civil Service, 31-2, 36.
  Colonial Administration, 33, 34-5, 39, 57-8, 61, 70, 82-3.
  Indian Civil Service, 33, 34-5, 39.
  Industrial Revolution, 52-3.
  Monarchy, 15.
  Parliamentary Government, 16, 22, 32.
  Universities, 23.
British Commonwealth, 11.
British Empire, 16.
Burke, Edmund, 28.
Burma, 11, 19, 23, 28, 33, 37.

*Index*

Calcutta University, 23.
Cambodia, 11, 17, 33.
Capital, Lack of, 45, 47.
Cervantes, 63.
Ceylon, 11, 19-20, 23, 33, 37.
CHINA, 32, 48.
  Education, 70.
  Industrialisation, 38, 46.
  Monarchy, 17-18.
  Railway Concessions, 79.
  Social Changes, 13-14, 90-1.
Cinema, 88, 89-90.
CIVIL SERVICE (see also Administration).
  in Britain, 31-2, 36.
  in India, 33, 34-5, 36, 37, 38-9.
  Need for Technical Personnel, 34, 36, 38-9.
  and Parliament, 39-41.
  as Stabilising Factor, 41-2.
COLONIAL GOVERNMENT.
  Administration, 32-5.
  Education, 57-8, 59-61, 70.
  in India, 21, 33-5, 39, 57-8, 70.
  and the Social Structure, 81, 82-3.
Communications, 45, 46, 89.
Communism, 46, 53, 92.

Community and the State, 13, 87-8.
Community Projects (India), 36, 50, 53-4, 88.
Confucianism, 13-14, 90-1.
Corneille, Pierre, 63.
Cromwell, Oliver, 29.

Delhi School of Economics, 23.
DEMOCRACY (see also Parliamentary Government). 26-7.
  Conception of Freedom, 26-7.
  Doctrine of Obedience, 17-20, 35.
  Importance of Education, 58-9, 63-4.
  Lack of Local Tradition, 15.
  Lack of Understanding, 17, 24-6, 27, 29-30, 35.
  and Local Government, 21.
  Party Organisation, 27-8.
  Principle of Equality, 26-7.
  Role of Universities, 22-3.
  and Social Reform, 27, 84-5.
  Sovereignty of Parliament, 29-30.
Dicey, A. V.: *Law of the Constitution*, 31-2; *Legislation and Public*

*Index*

*Opinion in England in the 19th Century*, 22.
Dollfuss, 16.

Ecole des Sciences Politiques, 23.
Economic Assistance, Foreign, 47-8, 50.
ECONOMY (see also Industrial and Rural Development).
under Colonial Rule, 44, 55.
Foreign Assistance, 47-8.
Lack of Capital, 45, 47.
Reorganisation in the new States, 37-8, 44 ff.
State Planning, 45-7.
EDUCATION.
Adult Education, 63-4.
in China, 70.
under Colonial Rule, 57-8, 59-61, 70.
and Democracy, 58-9, 63-4.
Illiteracy, 58, 63, 66.
in India, 57-8, 60, 63-5, 66, 70, 74-6.
in Indonesia, 57.
International Assistance, 66-8.
in Japan, 70.
Language Problems, 57-8, 61-3.
Missionary Activities, 66-7.
Primary Education, 64.
Scientific and Technical Training, 59, 61, 62-3, 65, 70-1, 74-6, 78.
Secondary Education, 64.
in the Sudan, 57-8.
Universities, 23, 64-5.
EGYPT, 11, 28-9, 30, 32.
Education, 64, 66.
Rural Development, 54.
Social Reform, 87.
Electricity Supply in India, 54.
Emancipation of Women, 82, 91-2, 94.
England, see Britain.
English Language in Education, 57-8, 61.
Ethiopia, 66.
EUROPE.
Evolution of Administration, 31-2.
Industrial Revolution, 69.
Monarchies, 15, 31.
Social Changes, 81-2.
Totalitarian Governments, 16.

Fabian Society, 22.
Family, see Social Structure.
Five Year Plans (India), 50-1, 54, 74-5.

*Index*

Foreign Economic Assistance, 47-8, 50.
FRANCE, 15, 16, 63.
   Colonial Administration, 33, 58.
   Parliamentary Government, 22.
   Universities, 23.
Franco, General, 16.
Frederick the Great, 62.
French Language in Education, 58, 61.
French Revolution, 81.

Gandhi, Mahatma, 60, 91.
German Language, 62.
Germany, 15, 22-3, 24, 76.
Ghana, 11.
Gokhale, Gopal Krishna, 58.
Gokhale School of Politics, (Poona), 23.
Great Rebellion in India (1857-58), 82.
Greece, 16.

Habsburgs, 16.
Hindi, 61, 62.
Hinduism, 82-3, 86.
Hiroshima, 12.
Hitler, Adolf, 16.
Hohenzollerns, 16.
Holland, 15, 37, 57, 61.
House of Commons, 20-1.
Humboldt, Wilhelm, Freiherr von, 22.

Hydro-electric Development in India, 49.

Ikwan ul Mussalmeen, 87.
Illiteracy, 58, 63, 66.
India, Ancient, 15, 32.
INDIA.
   Agriculture, 50, 53-4.
   under British Rule, 33, 34-5, 39, 70, 82-3.
   Capitalist Class, 49, 50-1.
   Caste System, 14, 27, 83, 86.
   Civil Service, 33, 34-5, 36, 37, 38-9, 40-1.
   Constitution, 85.
   Education, 57-8, 60, 63-5, 66, 70, 74-6.
   Industrial Development, 36-7, 38, 49-52, 89.
   Local Government, 21.
   Missionary Institutions, 66.
   National Congress, 28.
   Natural Resources, 49, 75.
   Need for Technical Personnel, 36, 38-9, 74-6.
   Parliamentary Government, 19-20, 40-1.
   Rural Development, 36, 50, 53-4, 88.
   Scientific and Technical Training, 69-71, 74-7.
   Scientific Research, 75-7.

*Index*

Social Structure, 14, 82-3, 85-6, 90-1, 94.
State Planning, 38, 45.
Indian Institute of Science, 70.
Indian Mutiny, see Great Rebellion.
INDONESIA, 11, 16, 19, 21.
  Civil Services, 33, 37.
  under Colonial Rule, 33.
  Education, 57, 64.
  Parliamentary Government, 25, 30.
  Universities, 23.
INDUSTRIAL DEVELOPMENT see also Economy), 45-52, 55-6, 71-2, 73-6.
  in China, 38.
  Effect on Village Autonomy, 89, 92-3.
  in India, 36-7, 38, 49-52, 74-6.
  and Science, 71-2, 73-5.
  Shortage of Technical Personnel, 36, 38-9, 47, 48-9, 71, 74-6.
  and Technology, 72, 73-4, 76.
Industrial Revolution in Europe, 52-3, 69.
Institutes of Higher Technology (India), 76.
International Bank, 51.
Iqbal, Dr. Mahommed, 87.
Iran, 48.

Iraq, 23, 48, 55.
Islam, 82, 86-7, 95.
Islamic Brotherhood, 87.
Istiqlal (Morocco), 28.

Japan, 29, 62, 70, 79.
Japanese Language, 62.
Jordan, 11.

Kharagpur (Bengal), 76.
Khartoum, 58.
Kuomintang, 48.

Land Reform, 50.
Language Problems in Education, 57-8, 61-3.
Laos, 11, 17, 33.
*Law of the Constitution* (A. V. Dicey), 31-2.
Lebanon, 11, 66.
*Legislation and Public Opinion in England in the 19th Century* (A. V. Dicey), 22.
Libya, 15, 18, 37, 66.
Living Standards, 44-5, 46, 52-3, 71.
Local Government
  in India, 21.
  Lack of Tradition in New States, 21.
London School of Economics, 23.
Louis XIV, 63.

Madras University, 23.

# Index

*Mahabharata*, 18.
Malaria, 78.
Malaya, 23, 55.
Marx, Karl, 53.
Massachusetts, Institute of Technology, 76.
Massu, General, 29.
Metaxas, General, 16.
Mirza, President, 25.
Missionary Activities, 66-7.
Molière, 63.
MONARCHY, 15-16, 17-18, 20, 85.
  in Asia, 15, 17-18.
  in Europe, 15, 24.
Morocco, 11, 17, 28, 33, 58, 61.
Muslim League (Pakistan), 28.
Mussolini, Benito, 16.

Napoleon Bonaparte, 29.
National Congress (India), 28, 50, 53-4.
National Extension Services (India), 36, 88.
Nationalism, 95.
Natural Resources, 45, 46, 71, 75.
Nazim-ud-Din, 26.
Nehru, Jawahalral, 45.
Neo Dastur (Tunisia), 28.
Nepal, 79.
Non-co-operation Movement (India), 60.

Northern (Scandinavian) Countries, 15, 16.
Nuclear Science, 73, 76-7.

Oil, 55, 79.
Oil Royalties, 48.
Ottomans, 16, 21.

PAKISTAN
  under British Rule, 33.
  Civil Service, 37.
  Industrial Development, 52, 89.
  Muslim League, 28.
  Parliamentary Government, 19-20, 25-6.
  Rural Development, 54, 88.
  Universities, 23.
Parkinson's Law, 36.
PARLIAMENTARY GOVERNMENT (see also Democracy), 18-30, 39-41.
  in Britain, 16, 22, 24-5.
  in Ceylon, 19-20.
  in France, 22, 24-5.
  Function of Second Chamber, 19.
  in India, 19-20, 40-1.
  Majority Decisions, 18-20.
  in Pakistan, 19-20, 25-6.
  Role of Opposition, 20.
  Sovereignty of Parliament, 29-30, 39-40.
Party Organisations in the New States, 28-9.

*Index*

Peter the Great, 62.
Petroleum, 44.
Pilsudski, Marshal, 16.
Planck, Max, 11.
Planned Economy in the New States, 45-7.
Planning Commission (India), 45.
Poland, 16, 19.
Portugal, 15, 16.
Private Enterprise in the New States, 38.
Public Health, 45.
Punjab, 50.

Racine, Jean, 63.
Radio, 88.
Railways, 45, 79.
Raman, C. V., 70.
Religion and the Social Structure, 86-7, 94-5.
Ripon, Lord, 21.
Romanoffs, 16.
Royal Society (Britain), 71.
Rubber, 44, 55.
Rural Development, 36, 52-4, 56, 88.
Russia, Czarist (see also Soviet Union), 15, 45, 62.
Russian Language, 62.

Sadler Commission (India), 65.
Salazar, Dr. Antonio, 16.
Sarjeant, Dr., 58.
Saudi Arabia, 37, 48. 55, 66.
Scandinavia, see Northern Countries.
SCIENCE.
　Advances in Western Countries, 69, 79-80.
　in India, 69-71, 74-7.
　and Industry, 71-2, 73-5, 80.
　International Assistance, 77-9.
　in Japan, 70.
　Research, 70-1, 75-7.
　Scientific and Technical Training, 59, 61, 62-3, 65, 70-1, 74-7, 78.
Security Council, 19.
Shihakly, Colonel, 29.
Shipbuilding, 69-70.
Sieyès, Abbé, 46.
Sind, 50.
SOCIAL STRUCTURE.
　Caste System, 14, 27, 83, 86.
　Changes in Europe, 81-2.
　under Colonial Rule, 81, 82-3.
　Emancipation of Women, 91-2, 94.
　and the Family, 89-92.
　and Hinduism, 82-3, 86.
　in India, 14, 82-3, 85-6.
　Influence of Radio and Cinema, 88, 89-90.

*Index*

and Islam, 82, 86-7, 95.
the Middle Class, 93-4.
Need for Reform, 84-5.
and Nationalism, 95.
and Religion, 86-7, 94-5.
and Tradition, 81 ff.
Village Autonomy, 87-9.
Soviet Union, 45, 47.
Spain, 15, 16, 63.
State and Community, 13, 87-8.
Steel Industry, 46, 49, 51, 70.
Stein, Karl, Freiherr von, 22.
Sudan, 11, 33, 37.
Sugar, 44.
Sukarno, President, 25.
Switzerland, 16.
Syria, 11, 19, 23, 29-30.

Tata, Jamshedji, 70.
Tata Institute of Fundamental Research, 75.
Tata Power Development Schemes, 49.
Tea, 44, 55.
TECHNOLOGY.
  Advances in Western Countries, 69-70.
  in India, 69-70, 74-7, 78.
  and Industry, 72, 73-4, 76, 80.
  International Assistance, 77-9.
  in Japan, 70.
  Shortage of Technical Personnel, 38-9, 47, 48-9, 71, 74-6, 78-9.
  Technical and Scientific Training, 59, 61, 62-3, 65, 70-1, 74-7.
Textile Industry, 49.
Tradition, see Social Structure.
Tunisia, 11, 17, 28, 33, 58, 61.
Turkey, 87.

UNESCO, 77.
United Nations, 77, 80.
Universities, 23, 64-5.
USA, 22, 23, 32, 48, 64.

Vietnam, 11.
Village Aid Projects (Pakistan), 54, 88.

Wafd (Egypt), 28-9.
Weber, Max, 32.
Wittfogel, Karl von, 32.
World War, First, 15, 16.
World War, Second, 13, 16, 47, 71.

Yemen, 37, 66.
Yuan Shih-kai, General, 29.